WEEKNIGHT COOKING FOR TWO

WEEKNIGHT
cooking for two

100 Five-Ingredient
Super Simple Suppers

Kenzie Swanhart

ROCKRIDGE
PRESS

FOR JULIEN, MY OTHER HALF

contents

Introduction 9

1 BREAKFAST FOR DINNER 15

2 SALADS 27

3 SOUPS & SANDWICHES 39

4 VEGETARIAN 57

5 SEAFOOD 75

6 MEAT 87

7 POULTRY 105

8 DESSERTS 123

The Dirty Dozen & the Clean Fifteen 135

Conversion Tables 136

Dietary Preference Cheat Sheet 137

Recipe Index 142

Index 144

introduction

HOW MANY TIMES A WEEK DO YOU ASK YOURSELF OR YOUR SIGNIFICANT OTHER "WHAT'S FOR DINNER?"

only to fall back on ordering takeout—again? During the week we are often so busy trying to get everything done, that dinner becomes a source of stress and aggravation. It's a problem faced not only by couples, but by everyone who lives in a small household—from empty-nesters and college students, to young people living on their own for the first time. But I have good news: Cooking weeknight dinners for two doesn't have to be a daunting task.

Over the years, my fiancé and I have learned a lot about cooking for two. Our first apartment right out of college had a kitchen the size of a closet. When we cooked together, it meant one of us was at the stove in the kitchen while the other was chopping veggies in the living room. Without the space to cook elaborate dishes or store a lot of ingredients, we learned that less was more, and we figured out how to keep our recipes as simple as possible without sacrificing flavor.

We've gained a little bit of kitchen space with each subsequent apartment, and we now have a kitchen large enough to cook an extravagant dinner or even host over the holidays. Yet as our kitchen space has increased, so too has our busyness during the week, so we still regularly turn to quick and simple weeknight meals. Cooking in two-person portions means we can use fresh, wholesome ingredients with lots of flavor, and it keeps us from eating the same leftovers three days in a row. Cooking at home can also have a positive health effect—smaller portions mean fewer calories, less fat, and less sodium.

Weeknight Cooking for Two is filled with simple yet flavorful five-ingredient meals that can be cooked in 30 minutes or less. These recipes all rely on wholesome, nourishing ingredients and range from traditional classics and hearty salads and soups, to everyone's favorite breakfast-for-dinner meals. The recipes in this book are fun, creative, and perfect for every day of the week, and they come with some of my personal shortcuts to make preparation even easier. I've also included a bonus chapter of five-ingredient desserts at the end of the book for those nights when you have a bit more time or are just craving something sweet.

What are you waiting for? Grab your apron and your plus one because it's time to cook!

KITCHEN STAPLES CHECKLIST

There are three staples used in almost every recipe throughout this book: olive oil, sea salt, and freshly ground black pepper. And if I had to pick a fourth, it would be garlic.

To make a breeze of putting together your grocery list, the following is a checklist of additional staple ingredients used in many of the recipes.

DAIRY
- Coconut milk
- Feta cheese
- Goat cheese
- Greek yogurt
- Mozzarella cheese
- Parmesan cheese

FRUITS
- Apples
- Avocadoes
- Bananas
- Berries
- Grapes
- Lemons
- Limes
- Oranges
- Pears
- Tomatoes (cherry, grape, heirloom, and vine)

HEALTHY FATS
- Butter
- Coconut oil
- Olive oil
- Sesame oil

HERBS AND SPICES
- Basil
- Black pepper, freshly ground
- Cayenne pepper
- Chili powder
- Cilantro
- Cinnamon, ground
- Crushed red pepper flakes
- Cumin
- Ginger, ground
- Italian seasoning
- Oregano, dried
- Red curry paste
- Sea salt
- Smoked paprika
- Thyme, dried

LEGUMES AND BEANS
- Black beans
- Cannellini beans
- Edamame
- Garbanzo beans
- Green beans
- Red beans

NATURAL SWEETENERS
- Honey
- Pure maple syrup

NUTS AND SEEDS
- Almonds
- Chia seeds
- Pecans
- Pine nuts
- Sesame seeds
- Walnuts

PROTEIN
- Beef
- Chicken
- Cod
- Eggs
- Pork (including bacon and prosciutto)
- Salmon
- Scallops
- Shrimp
- Tuna, canned
- Turkey

WHOLE GRAINS
- Arborio rice
- Brown rice
- Quinoa

VEGETABLES
- Arugula
- Asparagus
- Bell peppers
- Broccoli
- Brussels sprouts
- Butternut squash
- Carrots
- Cauliflower
- Cucumbers
- Eggplant
- Garlic
- Ginger, fresh
- Jalapeño
- Kale
- Mushrooms (button, portobello, shiitake, wild, and white)
- Olives (black, Kalamata)
- Onions
- Parsley, fresh
- Romaine lettuce
- Russet potatoes
- Scallions
- Shallots
- Spaghetti squash
- Spinach
- Sweet potatoes
- Thyme, fresh
- Zucchini

OTHER PANTRY STAPLES
- Almond flour
- Balsamic vinegar
- Beef broth
- Chicken broth
- Crushed tomatoes, canned
- Diced tomatoes, canned
- Hummus
- Marinara sauce
- Pumpkin purée, canned
- Salsa
- Salsa verde
- Tamari
- Tahini
- Tapioca flour
- Tomato sauce, canned
- Vegetable broth
- White vinegar
- White wine

ALL THE EQUIPMENT YOU NEED

You don't need to have a kitchen full of fancy tools to cook for two. However, there are a few pieces of equipment that I consider essential for every home cook's kitchen.

CAST-IRON SKILLET A cast-iron skillet has a natural nonstick bottom, heats evenly, can be transferred to the oven, and will last forever if you care for it properly. Equally adept at sautéing veggies and searing meat, this tool is a must-have for every kitchen.

NONSTICK PAN While I often opt for my cast-iron skillet to sear and build flavor in my dishes, every kitchen needs at least one good nonstick pan. Nonstick cookware is easy to use and clean. Buy one for cooking eggs, pancakes, and other foods that are known to stick.

SHEET PAN Sheet pans are not new kitchen gadgets, but they have easily become one of my favorite. Their size and shape make them perfect for holding a lot of food, even a whole meal, while still enabling browning, which means you get all the yummy caramelized flavor with almost no effort. They're a win-win.

STOCK POT Put simply, a stock pot's primary purpose is to make stock. But the beauty of this simple kitchen staple is that it can double as pot for making soups, stews, and more. To get the most out of your stock pot, it should be large enough to hold a whole chicken and veggies with room to spare. You may also want to have some additional sizes available or a Dutch oven that can be transferred to the oven, but be sure to invest in a large stock pot first.

GLASS BAKING DISHES Glass baking dishes are perfect for roasting your meals in the oven and can also double as food storage containers. They're great for storing and reheating meals if you decide to prep in advance or double up a meal.

1

BREAKFAST
for dinner

Shakshuka 16

Baked Eggs in Mushroom Cups 17

Sweet Potato Hash with
Baked Eggs 18

Brussels Sprouts and
Bacon Hash 19

Mediterranean Veggie Frittata 20

Mushroom and Scallion Frittata 21

Poached Egg over Creamy Polenta
with Sautéed Spinach 22

Southwest Breakfast Scramble 23

Steak and Eggs 24

Banana Pancakes 25

SHAKSHUKA (OPPOSITE), PAGE 16

SHAKSHUKA

SERVES 2 • PREP TIME 5 minutes • COOK TIME 15 minutes

This Middle Eastern dish seems to be popping up everywhere these days—flooding our social media feeds, gracing the pages of food magazines, and even making its way into the menu of my neighborhood café. This one-pan meal is pretty to look at and even more delicious to eat. Traditionally a savory breakfast, Shakshuka also makes a filling dinner for two. Make it extra special by adding a dollop of Greek yogurt or some crumbled feta on top.

1 TABLESPOON EXTRA-VIRGIN OLIVE OIL
1 SMALL ONION, CHOPPED
2 GARLIC CLOVES, CHOPPED
SEA SALT
FRESHLY GROUND BLACK PEPPER
2 RED BELL PEPPERS, CORED AND THINLY SLICED
1 (15-OUNCE) CAN DICED TOMATOES, DRAINED
2 EGGS

1. In a medium nonstick pan, heat the olive oil over medium heat. Add the onion and sauté for 3 to 4 minutes. Add the garlic, season with salt and pepper, and cook for another minute.

2. Add the bell peppers and cook for another 5 minutes.

3. Add the diced tomatoes and bring to a simmer. Season with salt and pepper.

4. Use a spoon to make two divots in the tomato sauce, and crack one egg into each one. Cover and let the sauce simmer for about 5 minutes, or until the egg whites are cooked but the yolks aren't set.

5. Remove from the heat, season again with pepper and serve.

DID YOU KNOW? Shakshuka is traditionally seasoned with cumin, paprika, and cayenne pepper. Spice up your dish by adding ¼ teaspoon of each of these pantry staples to the tomato sauce before adding the eggs. You can also boost the protein in this dish by adding ground beef to the sauce.

BAKED EGGS IN MUSHROOM CUPS

SERVES 2 • PREP TIME 5 minutes • COOK TIME 25 minutes

Eggs baked in a muffin tray are a breakfast staple in our household because they are easy to prep in advance, and to grab on the go throughout the week. In this recipe, portobello mushrooms and prosciutto pair perfectly to turn this breakfast favorite to a satisfying dinner. Serve on a bed of arugula to sneak in some greens and up your presentation game.

4 PORTOBELLO MUSHROOM CAPS, CLEANED AND
    TRIMMED WITH GILLS REMOVED
2 TABLESPOONS EXTRA-VIRGIN OLIVE OIL
4 SLICES PROSCIUTTO
4 EGGS
FRESHLY GROUND BLACK PEPPER
FRESH PARSLEY, CHOPPED

Optional Add-in
1 CUP ARUGULA, FOR SERVING

1. Preheat the oven to 375°F.

2. Lightly coat the outside of the mushroom caps with olive oil. Line a sheet pan with aluminum foil, and arrange the mushroom caps face-up on the sheet.

3. Place one slice of prosciutto inside each mushroom cap, and crack one egg into each cup. Season with black pepper and the parsley.

4. Carefully place the sheet pan into the oven, and bake for 20 to 25 minutes, or until the eggs set.

SEASONAL SWAP: If portobello mushrooms are out of season or you can't find them at your local market, avocados and large tomatoes are great alternatives. Just omit the prosciutto and scoop out some of the flesh to make a divot large enough to fit the egg.

SWEET POTATO HASH *with* BAKED EGGS

SERVES 2 • PREP TIME 5 minutes • COOK TIME 25 minutes

Long before I wrote my cookbook Spiralize It!, I had been using veggie noodles as a guilt-free replacement for pasta. I soon found that spiralized fruits and veggies could be used as much more than noodle substitutes; they were also perfect for salad toppings, coleslaw, crispy shoestring fries, and even desserts. But perhaps my favorite way to use the spiralizer is to incorporate more veggies into my favorite breakfast dishes. In this recipe, spiralized sweet potatoes create a perfectly crispy hash for baked eggs.

1 SWEET POTATO, SPIRALIZED INTO
    SPAGHETTI NOODLES
2 TABLESPOONS EXTRA-VIRGIN OLIVE OIL
SEA SALT
FRESHLY GROUND BLACK PEPPER
2 EGGS

Optional Add-in
GREEN ONIONS, THINLY SLICED, FOR GARNISH

1. Preheat the oven to 425°F.

2. Divide the sweet potato noodles among two individual skillets or baking dishes. Toss with the olive oil and season with salt and pepper.

3. Place in the oven and roast for 20 minutes, or until the edges start to get crispy and browned.

4. Remove from the oven and make a divot in the sweet potato large enough to fit the egg.

5. Crack an egg into each and bake for an additional 5 minutes, or until the egg is cooked to desired doneness.

SEASONAL SWAP: When it's in season, you can use butternut squash instead of sweet potato. You can also use russet potatoes or parsnip if you choose.

BRUSSELS SPROUTS *and* BACON HASH

SERVES 2 • PREP TIME 5 minutes • COOK TIME 25 minutes

Brussels sprouts and bacon are my go-to side dish during the week because they are easy to prepare and get super crispy and delicious with little effort. This version is beefed up with onion and apple to make it more of a main dish. If you want to add some protein, top the hash with a fried egg or mix in some chicken.

3 STRIPS BACON

EXTRA-VIRGIN OLIVE OIL

½ ONION, SLICED

1 GARLIC CLOVE, MINCED

1 POUND BRUSSELS SPROUTS, ENDS TRIMMED
    AND HALVED

1 APPLE, CORED AND CUBED

SEA SALT

1. Preheat the oven to 375°F.

2. Place the bacon in a cold cast-iron skillet. Turn on the stove and cook over medium-low heat until it reaches desired crispiness. Place a paper towel on a plate. Remove the bacon from the skillet and set aside on the plate.

3. Add the onion and sauté for 3 to 4 minutes in the bacon grease. Add the garlic and cook for another minute.

4. Add the Brussels sprouts and sauté for 5 to 7 minutes, stirring occasionally, until soft.

5. While the Brussels sprouts are cooking, chop up the bacon.

6. Add the apple, stir, and cook for an additional 5 to 7 minutes. Add the bacon and mix well. Cook for another 2 minutes, or until the Brussels sprouts are softened.

SEASONAL SWAP: I absolutely love the sweetness of the apples in this hash, but if apples are out of season or you are craving something more savory, you can use sweet potato instead.

MEDITERRANEAN VEGGIE FRITTATA

SERVES 2 • PREP TIME 5 minutes • COOK TIME 20 minutes

Frittatas are usually my brunch go-to, but since we always have eggs, milk, and veggies on hand, they also make an effortless dinner on nights when we can't decide what to cook. You can easily customize the flavor of this dish by using whatever veggies you have on hand.

1 TABLESPOON EXTRA-VIRGIN OLIVE OIL

½ SMALL ONION, CHOPPED

1 HEIRLOOM TOMATO, SLICED

½ CUP PITTED AND SLICED LENGTHWISE
   BLACK OLIVES

4 EGGS

½ CUP FULL-FAT COCONUT MILK

SEA SALT

FRESHLY GROUND BLACK PEPPER

Optional Add-ins

½ CUP FRESH PARSLEY, CHOPPED

1. Preheat the oven to 400°F.

2. In a cast-iron skillet, heat the olive oil over medium heat. Add the onion and sauté for 3 to 4 minutes. Add the tomato and olives, and cook for another 5 minutes, stirring occasionally.

3. In a bowl, crack the eggs. Add the coconut milk and season with salt and pepper. Whisk together.

4. Pour the egg mixture into the skillet, making sure all the vegetables are evenly covered. Cook for 1 to 2 minutes.

5. When the egg starts to lift at the edges, remove the skillet from the stove and place it in the oven for 5 to 7 minutes, or until the eggs are set.

MUSHROOM *and* SCALLION FRITTATA

SERVES 2 • PREP TIME 5 minutes • COOK TIME 20 minutes

Normally my fiancé protests when I cook a breakfast dish for dinner, but when I recently suggested a homemade frittata filled with mushrooms and scallions, he was more than intrigued. He even ate mushrooms from the skillet when he thought I wasn't looking! This one-pan meal is now a favorite for us and often ends up on our dinner table. To really make this dish sensational, sprinkle goat cheese on top before serving.

1 TABLESPOON EXTRA-VIRGIN OLIVE OIL

1 CUP CAPPED AND SLICED SHIITAKE MUSHROOMS

6 SCALLIONS, CUT INTO 1½-INCH PIECES

4 EGGS

½ CUP FULL-FAT COCONUT MILK

SEA SALT

FRESHLY GROUND BLACK PEPPER

1. Preheat the oven to 400°F.

2. In a medium cast-iron skillet, heat the olive oil over medium heat. Add the mushrooms and scallions, and sauté for 5 to 7 minutes. When the veggies cook down, season with salt and pepper.

3. In a bowl, crack the eggs. Add the coconut milk to the eggs, and season with salt and pepper. Whisk together.

4. Pour the egg mixture into the skillet, making sure all the vegetables are evenly covered. Cook for 1 to 2 minutes.

5. When the edges start to lift away from the skillet, remove the skillet from the stove and place it in the oven for 5 to 7 minutes, or until the eggs are set.

SEASONAL SWAP: If you can't find scallions at the market or they look too wilted, caramelized onions are a great alternative and add a delicious depth of flavor to this dish.

POACHED EGG *over* CREAMY POLENTA *with* SAUTÉED SPINACH

SERVES 2 • PREP TIME 5 minutes • COOK TIME 20 minutes

Whenever eggs make an appearance on our dinner table, Julien always classifies it as breakfast. Regardless, I happen to think that this dish is filling and delicious no matter the time of day. Creamy polenta and fresh greens are the perfect complement to a poached egg. Don't be intimidated by the fancy name, all it takes to master this dish are just a few ingredients and five simple steps.

1 TABLESPOON EXTRA-VIRGIN OLIVE OIL,
    PLUS MORE FOR GARNISH

4 CUPS SPINACH

SEA SALT

FRESHLY GROUND BLACK PEPPER

2 CUPS WATER

½ CUP INSTANT POLENTA

¼ CUP PARMESAN CHEESE

2 LARGE EGGS

CRUSHED RED PEPPER FLAKES, FOR GARNISH

1. In a cast-iron skillet, heat the olive oil over medium-high heat. Add the spinach and cook, stirring occasionally, until the spinach is wilted. Season with salt and pepper, transfer to a colander, and press to remove excess liquid.

2. Meanwhile, in a large pot, bring the water to a boil. Reduce the heat to low and slowly whisk in the polenta. Continue to whisk until the polenta is thickened, about 3 minutes. Remove from the heat, stir in the Parmesan cheese, and season with salt and pepper.

3. In a straight-sided skillet, heat 2 inches of water over medium heat until a few bubbles break the surface and form a gentle simmer.

4. Gently crack one egg into the simmering water. Repeat with remaining egg and cook for 2 to 3 minutes, or until the whites are set. Remove the eggs using a slotted spoon, and transfer to a plate lined with paper towels to drain.

5. Divide the polenta, spinach, and eggs among two bowls, and season with salt and pepper. Sprinkle with crushed red pepper flakes and olive oil on top.

DID YOU KNOW? To ensure the egg whites firm up quickly, add 2 teaspoons of white vinegar to the simmering water before adding the eggs.

SOUTHWEST BREAKFAST SCRAMBLE

SERVES 2 • PREP TIME 5 minutes • COOK TIME 15 minute

I perfected the art of the scrambled egg at around the same time I mastered the art of boiling water for pasta. They are two cooking skills that are necessary for any college student. However, as I got more comfortable in the kitchen, I learned that I could customize my scrambled eggs with flavorful additions like meat or vegetables to make a quick and easy meal. In this recipe, the onion, peppers, and black beans add a Southwestern flair, but you can easily replace them with spinach and feta for a Mediterranean twist.

1 TABLESPOON EXTRA-VIRGIN OLIVE OIL

½ ONION, CHOPPED

2 RED BELL PEPPERS, CORED AND CHOPPED

1 (14-OUNCE) CAN BLACK BEANS, DRAINED
    AND RINSED

4 EGGS

2 TABLESPOONS FULL-FAT COCONUT MILK

SEA SALT

FRESHLY GROUND BLACK PEPPER

Optional Add-ins

HOT SAUCE, FOR GARNISH

FRESH SALSA, FOR GARNISH

CILANTRO, CHOPPED, FOR GARNISH

1. In a medium cast-iron skillet, heat the olive oil over medium heat. Add the onion and sauté for 3 to 4 minutes. Add the peppers and cook for another 5 minutes, stirring occasionally. Add the black beans, stir, and cook for another 1 to 2 minutes.

2. In a bowl, crack the eggs. Add the coconut milk to the eggs and season with salt and pepper. Whisk together.

3. Pour the egg mixture into the skillet, making sure all the vegetables are evenly covered. Cook for 4 to 5 minutes or until the egg reaches desired doneness, stirring to scramble.

STEAK *and* EGGS

SERVES 2 • PREP TIME 10 minutes • COOK TIME 20 minutes

When I think of breakfast for dinner or dinner for breakfast, Steak and Eggs is the dish that always comes to mind. Simple and delicious, this is a two-person dish perfect anytime of the day. If you want to get fancy, make a savory mushroom sauce to drizzle on top.

2 (6-OUNCE) FILET MIGNON STEAKS
SEA SALT
FRESHLY GROUND BLACK PEPPER
2 TABLESPOONS BUTTER
1 SHALLOT, THINLY SLICED
2 EGGS, POACHED

1. Season all sides of the steak with salt and pepper.

2. In a large cast-iron skillet, melt the butter over medium-high heat.

3. Place the steaks in the skillet and sear for 4 to 5 minutes, flip, then continue cooking for an additional 4 to 5 minutes for medium-rare steak. Remove the steak from the skillet, and set aside to rest for at least 5 minutes.

4. Place the shallots in the leftover butter and steak juices, and sauté for 5 to 7 minutes, or until they are browned and crispy.

5. Serve each steak on a plate, accompanied with the shallots and a poached egg. Season with salt and pepper.

DID YOU KNOW? For best results, allow the steak to come to room temperature after taking it out of the refrigerator, about 1 hour before cooking. Also keep in mind that searing time depends on the thickness of your steaks and the desired degree of cooking.

BANANA PANCAKES

SERVES 2 • PREP TIME 5 minutes • COOK TIME 10 minutes

I couldn't have a "Breakfast for Dinner" chapter in this book without including something sweet. And what is better than Banana Pancakes made with just a handful of ingredients? I like to enjoy these pancakes with a drizzle of maple syrup, but you can also top them with fruit and whipped cream, or mix a handful of chocolate chips into the batter if you have a serious sweet tooth like me.

1 CUP ALMOND FLOUR
PINCH OF SEA SALT
¼ TEASPOON GROUND CINNAMON
4 EGGS
1 TEASPOON PURE VANILLA EXTRACT
2 BANANAS, MASHED
1 TABLESPOON COCONUT OIL

1. In a large bowl combine the almond flour, salt, and cinnamon.

2. In a separate bowl, whisk together the eggs and vanilla extract. Mix the wet ingredients with the dry ingredients. Add the bananas and mix until well combined.

3. In a large cast-iron skillet, heat the coconut oil over medium heat. Once evenly heated, pour the batter into the skillet. Cook each pancake until you see bubbles on the surface, flip, and continue cooking for 2 to 3 minutes.

4. Continue working in batches until all the batter is used.

INGREDIENT SWAP: If you do not have almond flour in your pantry, you can substitute it with oat or whole wheat flour.

2

SALADS

Classic Chopped Salad 28

Shredded Brussels Sprouts and
Quinoa Salad 29

Roasted Harvest Veggie Salad 30

Apple-and-Walnut Spinach Salad 31

Grilled Romaine and Chicken
Caesar Salad 32

Chicken BLT Salad 33

Fall Cobb Salad 34

Traditional Greek Salad 35

Chinese Chicken Salad 36

Kale and Quinoa Salad 37

FALL COBB SALAD (OPPOSITE), PAGE 34

CLASSIC CHOPPED SALAD

SERVES 2 • PREP TIME 10 minutes

If you love salads, you have probably eaten your fair share of kale. But this Classic Chopped Salad is not your average kale salad. Tossed with crunchy radicchio, creamy avocado, and crisp apple, it's an explosion for your taste buds. With these flavors coming together in every bite, keep the dressing simple with just a little EVOO and lemon juice.

2 CUPS ROUGHLY CHOPPED KALE

2 CUPS ROUGHLY CHOPPED RADICCHIO

1 AVOCADO, PITTED, PEELED, AND CUBED

1 LARGE APPLE, CORED AND CHOPPED

2 TABLESPOONS EXTRA-VIRGIN OLIVE OIL

1 TABLESPOON FRESHLY SQUEEZED LEMON JUICE

SEA SALT

FRESHLY GROUND BLACK PEPPER

Optional Add-ins

2 TABLESPOONS RAW ALMONDS

2 SLICES BACON, CHOPPED

¼ CUP CRUMBLED BLUE CHEESE

1. In a large bowl, combine the kale, radicchio, avocado, and apple.

2. In a small bowl, whisk together the olive oil and lemon juice. Season with salt and pepper.

3. Drizzle the salad with the dressing and toss gently to coat evenly.

PAIR UP: To bulk up this salad as a main course, pile on the protein. Chopped chicken or leftover turkey complement the flavors well.

SHREDDED BRUSSELS SPROUTS *and* QUINOA SALAD

SERVES 2 • PREP TIME 10 minutes • COOK TIME 20 minutes

My favorite thing about food trends is how even the most hated vegetables can suddenly become popular. I didn't grow up eating Brussels sprouts, but once they started showing up on my favorite menus and magazines, I took notice and learned to cook them at home. I love how versatile these little veggies are—try roasting them with bacon (see Brussels Sprouts and Bacon Hash, page 19), tossing them into a pasta bowl with a creamy sauce, or shredding them, like in this salad!

½ CUP RED QUINOA, RINSED AND DRAINED

1 CUP WATER

JUICE OF 1 LEMON

1 TEASPOON LEMON ZEST

2 TABLESPOONS EXTRA-VIRGIN OLIVE OIL

1 POUND BRUSSELS SPROUTS, ENDS TRIMMED
    AND THINLY SLICED

¼ CUP CHOPPED WALNUTS

¼ CUP POMEGRANATE SEEDS

SEA SALT

1. In a large pot, add the quinoa and water and bring to a boil over high heat, stirring frequently. Reduce the heat to low and let simmer for 15 to 20 minutes, covered, stirring occasionally.

2. Once the liquid is absorbed and the quinoa is tender, remove the pot from the heat. Use a fork to fluff the quinoa, then transfer it to a large bowl and let cool.

3. In a small bowl, whisk the lemon juice, lemon zest, and olive oil together.

4. Add the Brussels sprouts, walnuts, and pomegranate seeds to the quinoa. Season with salt and drizzle with the dressing. Toss gently to coat evenly.

PAIR UP: To add even more flavor to your salad, replace the water with chicken or vegetable broth when cooking the quinoa.

ROASTED HARVEST VEGGIE SALAD

SERVES 2 • PREP TIME 10 minutes • COOK TIME 20 minutes

Salads can be so much more than a boring blend of chopped lettuce and cherry tomatoes. In fact, this roasted veggie combo has no lettuce at all! Once I realized salads don't have to fit the status quo, I started experimenting with all different kinds of veggies. Roasting all the vegetables before tossing them together, like in this recipe, is a delicious and super easy way to pull together a meal!

1 POUND BRUSSELS SPROUTS, ENDS TRIMMED
    AND HALVED
1 SWEET POTATO, CUBED
1 CUP SLICED BABY BELLA MUSHROOMS
2 TABLESPOONS EXTRA-VIRGIN OLIVE OIL
SEA SALT
FRESHLY GROUND BLACK PEPPER
¼ CUP TAHINI
2 GARLIC CLOVES, MINCED

Optional Add-ins
¼ CUP PINE NUTS
2 CUPS BABY KALE

1. Preheat the oven to 400°F.

2. In a large bowl, add the Brussels sprouts, sweet potato, mushrooms, and olive oil. Season with salt and pepper, and mix until well combined. Spread the mixture on a sheet pan lined with parchment paper, and bake for 20 minutes, flipping halfway through.

3. In a small bowl, combine the tahini and garlic to make the dressing.

4. Remove the vegetables from the oven. Drizzle with dressing and toss gently to coat evenly.

SEASONAL SWAP: When it's in season, butternut squash is a great alternative to sweet potato. You may need to increase the cook time slightly to ensure that the squash is fully cooked.

APPLE-*and*-WALNUT SPINACH SALAD

SERVES 2 • PREP TIME 15 minutes

The delicious combination of fresh greens, sliced fruit, and chopped nuts is a proven classic. I love spinach, apples, and walnuts in the fall, but you can just as easily use pears and pecans for a different flavor. Add even more texture with crumbled goat cheese and sliced onion, or pile on the protein by adding chicken or fish.

1 CUP BABY SPINACH, WASHED AND DRIED

1 APPLE, CORED AND THINLY SLICED

½ CUP HALVED AND TOASTED WALNUTS

⅓ CUP DRIED CRANBERRIES

2 TABLESPOONS EXTRA-VIRGIN OLIVE OIL

1 TABLESPOON FRESHLY SQUEEZED LEMON JUICE

SEA SALT

FRESHLY GROUND BLACK PEPPER

Optional Add-ins

¼ CUP CRUMBLED GOAT CHEESE

½ SMALL RED ONION, PEELED AND THINLY SLICED

1. In a large bowl, combine the spinach, apple, walnuts, and cranberries.

2. In a small bowl, whisk together the olive oil and lemon juice to make the dressing. Season with salt and pepper.

3. Drizzle the salad with the dressing and toss gently to coat evenly.

GRILLED ROMAINE and CHICKEN CAESAR SALAD

SERVES 2 • PREP TIME 10 minutes • COOK TIME 15 minutes

This Caesar salad is anything but ordinary. By grilling the lettuce, you can take this familiar salad to another level without much effort. While the recipe outlines the technique for making this dish on the stove, I love to prepare the romaine and chicken on the grill. In fact, we eat this salad about once a week in the summer when we can grill and eat out on our deck. Pair this salad with a glass of white wine for a light and refreshing meal for two on a warm summer evening.

2 TABLESPOONS EXTRA-VIRGIN OLIVE OIL, DIVIDED

½ POUND CHICKEN BREAST, THINLY CUT

SEA SALT

FRESHLY GROUND BLACK PEPPER

1 HEAD ROMAINE LETTUCE, TOPS AND BOTTOMS
    TRIMMED, CUT LENGTHWISE INTO QUARTERS

CAESAR DRESSING

2 TABLESPOONS GRATED PARMESAN CHEESE

1. In a medium cast-iron skillet, heat 1 tablespoon of olive oil over medium heat. Season the chicken with salt and pepper, and grill each side for 3 to 4 minutes, or until fully cooked. Transfer to a cutting board and slice.

2. Heat the grill or a grill pan to medium heat. Drizzle the remaining olive oil over the lettuce. Grill the lettuce for 15 to 20 seconds on each side, or until it is lightly golden.

3. Divide the lettuce between two plates, add the grilled chicken, drizzle with the Caesar dressing, and sprinkle with the Parmesan cheese.

DID YOU KNOW? Caesar dressing is quick and easy to make at home. In a blender or food processor, blend 2 tablespoons of homemade mayonnaise (see the tip on page 49), 2 teaspoons of Dijon mustard, 2 pressed garlic cloves, and ¼ cup of freshly squeezed lemon juice. Season with salt and pepper, add ¼ cup of Parmesan cheese, and pulse again.

CHICKEN BLT SALAD

SERVES 2 • PREP TIME 20 minutes

Everyone loves a good BLT sandwich. It is easy to throw together with just a few simple ingredients and is always packed with flavor. This salad turns a traditional BLT on its head by tossing out the bread and adding grilled chicken for a protein-packed dinner. Want to add even more flavor and texture? Try adding creamy avocado and your favorite nuts or seeds for extra crunch!

4 CUPS MIXED GREENS

½ POUND BONELESS CHICKEN BREAST, GRILLED
    AND SLICED

4 SLICES BACON, COOKED AND CHOPPED

2 EGGS, HARDBOILED

½ CUP CHERRY TOMATOES, HALVED

1 TO 2 TABLESPOONS EXTRA-VIRGIN OLIVE OIL

Optional Add-ins

1 AVOCADO, DICED

SESAME SEEDS, FOR GARNISH

SUNFLOWER SEEDS, FOR GARNISH

1. In a large bowl, combine the mixed greens, chicken, bacon, eggs, and tomatoes.

2. Drizzle with the olive oil and toss gently to coat evenly.

FALL COBB SALAD

SERVES 2 • PREP TIME 20 minutes

There is no single way to make a Cobb salad, but every version counts on one detail: The salad is always topped with neat little rows of veggies and protein, making it fun to assemble. During the week, we forage through the fridge and top the lettuce with whatever we have on hand. This version is my fiancé Julien's personal favorite whenever we have fresh apples lying around. Although you can make this salad with just five ingredients, it really wouldn't be Julien's favorite without adding some crumbled goat cheese on top.

4 CUPS CHOPPED ROMAINE LETTUCE

4 SLICES BACON, COOKED AND CHOPPED

2 EGGS, HARDBOILED

1 LARGE APPLE, DICED

½ CUP HALVED PECANS

1 TO 2 TABLESPOONS EXTRA-VIRGIN OLIVE OIL

Optional Add-ins

¼ CUP DRIED CRANBERRIES

¼ CUP CRUMBLED GOAT CHEESE

1. Fill a large bowl with the romaine lettuce.

2. Arrange the bacon, eggs, apple, and pecans on top of the romaine lettuce in neat rows.

3. Drizzle with the olive oil and serve.

DID YOU KNOW? For perfect hardboiled eggs, place the eggs in a single layer at the bottom of a pot. Cover with cold water, exceeding the height of the eggs by 1 inch. Cover the pot and bring the water to a boil. Then remove the pot from the heat and keep covered. Let the eggs stand for 12 minutes.

TRADITIONAL GREEK SALAD

SERVES 2 • PREP TIME 10 minutes

When I used to work in downtown Boston, my coworkers and I often lunched at a little Mediterranean restaurant nearby. My favorite thing on their menu was the Greek salad. Different from most Greek salads I've had, this one was filled with only chopped veggies and dressed with olive oil—not a lettuce leaf in sight. I knew Julien would love this salad too, so I re-created it at home. It quickly became our go-to for an easy weeknight meal.

1 ENGLISH CUCUMBER, CHOPPED

½ CUP HALVED CHERRY TOMATOES

1 RED ONION, THINLY SLICED

¼ CUP PITTED AND HALVED KALAMATA OLIVES

¼ CUP CRUMBLED FETA CHEESE

FRESHLY GROUND BLACK PEPPER

1 TO 2 TABLESPOONS EXTRA-VIRGIN OLIVE OIL

Optional Add-in

4 CUPS ROMAINE LETTUCE, ROUGHLY CHOPPED

1. In a large bowl, combine the cucumber, tomatoes, onion, olives, and feta cheese.

2. Drizzle with the olive oil, season with pepper, and toss gently to coat evenly.

PAIR UP: Chickpeas are packed with protein and make a delicious addition to any Greek salad. Serve them straight from the can (drained and rinsed) or roast them for a little extra crunch.

CHINESE CHICKEN SALAD

SERVES 2 • PREP TIME 20 minutes

Filled with fresh and colorful vegetables, my Chinese Chicken Salad is a feast for the eyes as well as the stomach. This is one of my all-time favorite recipes; I absolutely love the bright colors and the satisfying crunch! Top with a drizzle of olive oil to keep things simple or add some extra flair with the vinaigrette recipe I provided in the tip.

4 CUPS CHOPPED ROMAINE LETTUCE

2 CUPS COOKED AND THINLY SLICED
    CHICKEN BREAST

1 CUP SHREDDED RED CABBAGE

¼ CUP SHREDDED CARROTS

¼ CUP EDAMAME

1 TO 2 TABLESPOONS OF EXTRA-VIRGIN OLIVE OIL

Optional Add-ins

1 GREEN ONION, THINLY SLICED

¼ CUP SLICED ALMONDS

1. In a large bowl, combine the lettuce, chicken, cabbage, carrots, and edamame.

2. Drizzle with the olive oil and toss gently to coat evenly.

PAIR UP: For an extra kick of flavor, before dressing the salad combine the olive oil with ½ teaspoon of minced garlic, 1 tablespoon of tamari, 2 teaspoons of rice vinegar, and ½ teaspoon of toasted sesame oil.

KALE *and* QUINOA SALAD

SERVES 2 • PREP TIME 10 minutes • COOK TIME 20 minutes

Quinoa is an easy and delicious way to bulk up a simple salad without making it too heavy, not to mention that the seed is packed with nutrients. Here chopped kale complements the quinoa's natural nuttiness, a sunny lemon dressing brightens up the dish, and pecans add an extra crunch. As with all the other salads in this chapter, adding in a little extra protein will also bulk it up so that you are not left feeling deprived.

½ CUP QUINOA, RINSED AND DRAINED

1 CUP WATER

JUICE OF 1 LEMON

1 TEASPOON LEMON ZEST

2 TABLESPOONS EXTRA-VIRGIN OLIVE OIL

4 CUPS CHOPPED KALE

1 AVOCADO, PITTED, PEELED, AND DICED

½ CUP CHOPPED PECANS

Optional Add-in

¼ CUP CRUMBLED GOAT CHEESE

1. In a large pot, add the quinoa and water and bring to a boil over high heat, stirring frequently. Reduce the heat to low and let simmer for 15 to 20 minutes, stirring occasionally.

2. Once the liquid is absorbed and the quinoa is tender, remove from the heat. Use a fork to fluff the quinoa, transfer it into a large bowl, and let it cool.

3. In a small bowl, whisk together the lemon juice, lemon zest, and olive oil.

4. Add the kale, avocado, and pecans to the quinoa. Season with salt and drizzle with the lemon dressing. Toss gently to coat evenly.

3

SOUPS
& sandwiches

Cream of Broccoli Soup   40

Creamy Tomato Soup   41

Wild Mushroom Soup   42

Pumpkin-Coconut Soup   43

Black Bean Soup   44

White Chicken Chili   45

Cauliflower and Celeriac Soup   46

Creamy Vegetable Soup   47

Carrot and Ginger Soup   48

Chicken Club Wrap   49

Tuna and Avocado Wrap   50

Chicken Salad Lettuce Wrap   51

Eggplant, Avocado, and
Bacon Roll-up   52

Portobello Philly Cheesesteak   53

Classic Burger   54

CREAMY TOMATO SOUP (OPPOSITE), PAGE 41

CREAM of BROCCOLI SOUP

SERVES 2 • PREP TIME 5 minutes • COOK TIME 25 minutes

Soup is always a comforting way to end a winter day. Canned soup is loaded with preservatives and salt, so I prefer to make my own. All you need is a large stock pot (see All the Equipment You Need, page 12), an immersion blender, and 30 minutes. The best part is that even though this recipe takes about 30 minutes, the stove is doing the work most of that time. If you don't have an immersion blender, you can transfer the soup to a traditional blender pitcher for the same smooth texture.

1 HEAD BROCCOLI, COARSELY CHOPPED

½ HEAD CAULIFLOWER, COARSELY CHOPPED

½ WHITE ONION, CHOPPED

2 CUPS VEGETABLE BROTH

½ CUP FULL-FAT COCONUT MILK

SEA SALT

FRESHLY GROUND BLACK PEPPER

Optional Add-ins

CHEDDAR CHEESE, SHREDDED, FOR GARNISH

GREEK YOGURT, FOR GARNISH

1. In a large pot over high heat, bring the broccoli, cauliflower, onion, vegetable broth, and coconut milk to a boil. Season with salt and pepper. Reduce the heat to low, and cook for 20 minutes.

2. Remove from the heat and blend using an immersion blender until smooth.

CREAMY TOMATO SOUP

SERVES 2 • PREP TIME 5 minutes • COOK TIME 25 minutes

Tomato soup is hands-down my all-time favorite soup. Whether in the middle of winter or the dead of summer, tomato soup can cure just about any woe and make you feel warm and fuzzy inside. The coconut milk in this recipe makes the soup extra creamy, but if you prefer a classic tomato soup, simply omit the coconut milk and blend until you reach your desired consistency.

1 (28-OUNCE) CAN CRUSHED TOMATOES

½ CUP VEGETABLE BROTH

½ CUP COCONUT MILK

2 TABLESPOONS BUTTER

SEA SALT

FRESHLY GROUND BLACK PEPPER

Optional Add-ins

OLIVE OIL, FOR GARNISH

FRESH BASIL, FOR GARNISH

CRUSHED RED PEPPER FLAKES, FOR GARNISH

1. In a large pot over high heat, bring the crushed tomatoes, vegetable broth, coconut milk, and butter to a boil. Reduce the heat to medium-low, and cook for 30 minutes. Season the soup with salt and pepper.

2. Remove from the heat. Blend using an immersion blender until smooth, and serve. For extra flavor, top with a drizzle of olive oil, and sprinkle with basil and red pepper flakes.

SEASONAL SWAP: If tomatoes are in season and you have a little bit of extra time, try substituting the canned crushed tomatoes with roasted fresh tomatoes.

WILD MUSHROOM SOUP

SERVES 2 • PREP TIME 5 minutes • COOK TIME 30 minutes

If there is a mushroom dish on the menu when we go out, chances are Julien's going to order it. He's the biggest mushroom fan I know. In fact, I don't remember particularly liking mushrooms until I met him. I didn't hate them; I just kind of avoided them. Nowadays they frequently appear on our dinner table. This soup is a simple way to enjoy the flavor of wild mushrooms without too many frills.

1 TABLESPOON EXTRA-VIRGIN OLIVE OIL

1 SHALLOT, DICED

4 CUPS SLICED WILD MUSHROOMS

½ TABLESPOON FRESH THYME

3 CUPS CHICKEN BROTH

½ CUP FULL-FAT COCONUT MILK

SEA SALT

FRESHLY GROUND BLACK PEPPER

Optional Add-in

¼ CUP CHOPPED FRESH PARSLEY FOR GARNISH

1. In a large pot, heat the olive oil over medium-high heat. Add the shallot and sauté for 3 to 4 minutes.

2. Add the mushrooms and thyme and cook for 5 minutes.

3. Add the chicken broth and bring to a boil. Reduce the heat and simmer for 15 minutes. Stir in the coconut milk, season with salt and pepper, and let simmer for 5 minutes.

PAIR UP: If you prefer a thicker soup, add 1 to 2 tablespoons of tapioca starch before serving, stirring until the soup reaches your desired consistency.

PUMPKIN-COCONUT SOUP

SERVES 2 • PREP TIME 5 minutes • COOK TIME 15 minutes

Coconut milk gives this soup a velvety texture, while the combination of red curry and ginger add bold flavor. The result is a delicious Thai-inspired soup. Creamy and comforting, this recipe is sure to keep you warm on even the coldest of nights. Looking for something with a bit more texture? Stir in your favorite veggies or pour this soup on top of chicken and rice for a quick and easy pumpkin-coconut curry.

1 TABLESPOON RED CURRY PASTE

½ TEASPOON GROUND GINGER

2 CUPS VEGETABLE BROTH

1 (15-OUNCE) CAN PUMPKIN PURÉE

½ CUP FULL-FAT COCONUT MILK

Optional Add-ins

ROASTED PEPITAS, FOR GARNISH

RED CHILE PEPPER, SLICED FOR GARNISH

FRESH CILANTRO, CHOPPED, FOR GARNISH

1. In a medium pot over high heat, cook the curry paste and ground ginger for about 1 minute, or until the paste becomes fragrant. Add the vegetable broth and pumpkin purée, and bring to a boil, stirring occasionally.

2. Reduce the heat to medium-low, add the coconut milk, and cook for 10 minutes, stirring occasionally.

BLACK BEAN SOUP

SERVES 2 • PREP TIME 5 minutes • COOK TIME 15 minutes

This might be one of the simplest recipes in the whole book—but it is also one of the tastiest! The black beans make this soup filling without being too heavy. And when the beans are combined with chicken broth and diced tomatoes, the three ingredients come together to create a hearty soup packed with flavor. This is the perfect weeknight meal because you probably already have these common ingredients in the pantry.

1 (15.5-OUNCE) CAN BLACK BEANS

½ CUP CHICKEN BROTH

1 (7-OUNCE) CAN DICED TOMATOES

Optional Add-ins

½ JALAPEÑO, DICED, FOR GARNISH

1 TABLESPOON GREEN ONIONS, THINLY SLICED, FOR GARNISH

1. In a medium pot over high heat, bring the black beans, chicken broth, and diced tomatoes to a boil. Reduce the heat to medium, and simmer for 10 minutes.

2. Remove from the heat and blend using an immersion blender.

DID YOU KNOW? There are many varieties of canned diced tomatoes! To kick up the flavor of this recipe, use diced tomatoes with green chiles.

WHITE CHICKEN CHILI

SERVES 2 • PREP TIME 5 minutes • COOK TIME 20 minutes

While I'm a fan of a good bowl of traditional chili, I also like to change it up. This version allows you to use chicken left over from another meal, adding beans and a few other kitchen staples to create a whole new meal! Make it your own with a variety of garnishes or some homemade tortilla chips on the side.

2 CUPS LEFTOVER ROTISSERIE CHICKEN

3 CUPS CHICKEN BROTH

1 (15-OUNCE) CAN CANNELLINI BEANS, DRAINED

1 CUP SALSA VERDE

1 TEASPOON GROUND CUMIN

SEA SALT

FRESHLY GROUND BLACK PEPPER

Optional Add-ins

AVOCADO, SLICED, FOR GARNISH

FRESH CILANTRO, CHOPPED, FOR GARNISH

1. In a medium pot over medium-high heat, heat the chicken, chicken broth, beans, salsa verde, and cumin. Season with salt and pepper.

2. Once the chili comes to a boil, turn the heat down to low and let simmer for 10 to 15 minutes.

DID YOU KNOW? Salsa verde is a green salsa made from tomatillos instead of tomatoes. The tomatillos add tanginess, while the chiles add a hot bite. Want even more heat? Add some diced jalapeño to the recipe.

CAULIFLOWER *and* CELERIAC SOUP

SERVES 2 • PREP TIME 10 minutes • COOK TIME 25 minutes

Perhaps one of the most versatile vegetables, cauliflower has earned a permanent spot on my grocery list. Whether I am roasting it for a salad, ricing it for pizza crust, or puréeing it into a soup, cauliflower is incorporated into at least one meal a week in our house. In this recipe, cauliflower is paired with celeriac, or celery root, a lesser-known vegetable with a distinctly bold flavor you are sure to fall in love with.

1 TABLESPOON EXTRA-VIRGIN OLIVE OIL

2 GARLIC CLOVES, CHOPPED

1 SMALL HEAD CAULIFLOWER

1 CUP PEELED AND CHOPPED CELERIAC

2 CUPS CHICKEN BROTH

2 TABLESPOONS BUTTER

SEA SALT

FRESHLY GROUND BLACK PEPPER

Optional Add-in

1 TABLESPOON FRESH CHIVES, FOR GARNISH

1. In a large pot, heat the olive oil over medium-high heat. Add the garlic and sauté for 1 to 2 minutes, or until brown.

2. Cut the head of the cauliflower into small florets. Add the cauliflower florets, celeriac, and chicken broth to the pot. Cover, reduce the heat, and simmer for 15 to 20 minutes, or until vegetables are tender.

3. Add the butter and stir. Season with the salt and pepper.

4. Remove from the heat and blend using an immersion blender until smooth.

CREAMY VEGETABLE SOUP

SERVES 2 • PREP TIME 5 minutes • COOK TIME 30 minutes

Homemade soups come in all kinds of varieties and consistencies. A traditional vegetable soup usually has a thinner broth with lots of veggies, but sometimes nothing beats a nice, creamy soup—especially in the colder months. You'll love the bright and inviting orange color that the carrots and sweet potato give this soup. And the hearty taste will have you and your partner coming back for seconds.

2 CARROTS, PEELED AND CHOPPED

1 CELERY STALK, CHOPPED

1 SWEET POTATO, PEELED AND CHOPPED

2 RUSSET POTATOES, PEELED AND CHOPPED

2 CUPS VEGETABLE BROTH

1. In a medium pot over high heat, bring the carrots, celery, sweet potato, russet potatoes, and vegetable broth to a boil. Reduce the heat to medium and simmer for 25 minutes, or until the vegetables are fully cooked and tender.

2. Remove from the heat and blend using an immersion blender until smooth.

CARROT *and* GINGER SOUP

SERVES 2 • PREP TIME 5 minutes • COOK TIME 25 minutes

If you're feeling under the weather, this is the soup for you. The carrots and ginger are packed with nutrients, and the warmth of the soup is sure to leave you feeling cozy. The rich taste of the coconut milk balances out the zing of the ginger, and the roasted carrots add a nice boost of flavor to this delicious, super-simple meal.

3 CARROTS, PEELED AND CHOPPED

2 TABLESPOONS EXTRA-VIRGIN OLIVE OIL, DIVIDED

SEA SALT

FRESHLY GROUND BLACK PEPPER

1 SMALL YELLOW ONION, DICED

2 TABLESPOONS MINCED FRESH GINGER

2 CUPS VEGETABLE BROTH

¼ CUP FULL-FAT COCONUT MILK

1. Preheat the oven to 400°F.

2. In a large bowl, combine the carrots and 1 tablespoon of olive oil. Season with salt and pepper and toss to coat. Spread the carrots in a single layer on a sheet pan lined with foil. Cook for 15 minutes, flipping halfway through.

3. In a large pot, heat the remaining olive oil over medium-high heat. Add the onion and sauté for 4 to 5 minutes. Add the ginger and vegetable broth, and bring to a boil. Reduce the heat, cover, and let simmer for 4 to 5 minutes, or until the ginger is tender. Add the carrots and coconut milk to the pot.

4. Remove from the heat and blend using an immersion blender until smooth.

DID YOU KNOW? I love using fresh ginger, but I rarely use the entire root before it dries up in my cupboard or fridge. Freezing ginger will not only extend its shelf life by months, it will also make it easier to peel and grate since fresh, unfrozen ginger tends to separate into stringy fibers.

CHICKEN CLUB WRAP

SERVES 2 • PREP TIME 10 minutes • COOK TIME 10 minutes

This wrap is proof that even an old classic can be made new with a few simple tricks. I've cleaned up this deli classic by substituting the carb-filled bread with lettuce, and opting for fresh, grilled chicken over the deli variety. Say good-bye to heavy sandwiches that leave you feeling sluggish, and hello to a wrap that is sure to fuel you for whatever evening tasks you have planned.

1 TABLESPOON EXTRA-VIRGIN OLIVE OIL

½ POUND BONELESS, SKINLESS CHICKEN BREAST

SEA SALT

FRESHLY GROUND BLACK PEPPER

4 LARGE ROMAINE LETTUCE LEAVES

2 TABLESPOONS MAYONNAISE

1 TOMATO, SLICED

4 STRIPS BACON, COOKED AND CRUMBLED

Optional Add-in

1 AVOCADO, CHOPPED

1. In a medium cast-iron skillet, heat the olive oil over medium heat. Season the chicken with salt and pepper, and grill each side for 3 to 4 minutes, or until fully cooked. Transfer to a cutting board and slice.

2. Divide the lettuce leaves between two plates, and assemble the wraps by topping the lettuce leaves with the chicken, mayonnaise, tomato, and bacon.

DID YOU KNOW? Most store-bought mayonnaise is packed with preservatives and artificial ingredients. I like to make my own by combining egg, oil, vinegar, Dijon mustard, salt, and lemon juice. Don't have time to make your own? Choose a mayo brand with just a few simple ingredients, and make sure you can pronounce them all!

TUNA and AVOCADO WRAP

SERVES 2 • PREP TIME 10 minutes

There are some foods that inarguably belong together: peanut butter and jelly, ham and cheese, or tuna and mayo, to name a few. But this delicious spin on the tuna-and-mayo combo is sure to please even the most die-hard fan of the classic tuna sandwich. Instead of mayonnaise, smother your tuna with creamy avocado and add some jalapeño for a little extra kick.

½ RIPE AVOCADO

1 TABLESPOON LIME JUICE

1 (5-OUNCE) CAN TUNA, DRAINED

½ JALAPEÑO, SEEDS REMOVED, THINLY SLICED

SEA SALT

FRESHLY GROUND BLACK PEPPER

4 BUTTER LETTUCE LEAVES, FOR SERVING

1. In a large bowl, mash the avocado. Add the lime juice and continue to mash until well combined.

2. Add the tuna and jalapeño to the avocado mixture and mix to combine, breaking up the tuna with a fork. Season with salt and pepper.

3. Divide the tuna between the lettuce leaves and roll into a wrap.

SEASONAL SWAP: If you are not grain-free, you can use whole wheat wraps instead of lettuce.

CHICKEN SALAD LETTUCE WRAP

SERVES 2 • PREP TIME 10 minutes

I bet that if you asked a bunch of friends for their chicken salad recipes, each person would give you a different recipe. Everyone likes to put their own spin on chicken salad. This version is my personal favorite. I love the way the juicy grapes balance out the crunch of the celery. Using butter lettuce to wrap up the salad results in a meal for two that is not only light yet satisfying, but also easy to pull together on even the busiest of nights.

2 CUPS CHOPPED COOKED CHICKEN

½ CUP HALVED GRAPES

1 CELERY STALK, CHOPPED

½ CUP HOMEMADE MAYONNAISE

SEA SALT

FRESHLY GROUND BLACK PEPPER

4 BUTTER LETTUCE LEAVES, FOR SERVING

Optional Add-ins

½ SMALL APPLE, PEELED AND CHOPPED

¼ CUP CHOPPED RED ONION

¼ CUP CHOPPED PECANS

1. In a large bowl, combine the chicken, grapes, celery, and mayonnaise. Season with salt and pepper, and mix until well combined.

2. Divide the chicken salad evenly between the lettuce leaves, and roll into a wrap.

EGGPLANT, AVOCADO, *and* BACON ROLL-UP

SERVES 2 • PREP TIME 10 minutes • COOK TIME 15 minutes

Avocado and arugula may start with the same letter, but they couldn't be farther apart on the flavor spectrum! I love bringing them together in this unexpected pairing. Eggplant makes a flavorful and filling base, and the crunch of bacon is just as delicious as it is unexpected. This fun roll-up is easy to make, but it looks like something out of a fancy restaurant menu and is sure to impress your other half.

1 TABLESPOON OLIVE OIL

1 MEDIUM EGGPLANT, THINLY SLICED

½ AVOCADO, THINLY SLICED

4 STRIPS BACON, COOKED AND CHOPPED

1 CUP ARUGULA

SEA SALT

FRESHLY GROUND BLACK PEPPER

1. In a large cast-iron skillet, heat the olive oil over medium heat. Add the eggplant slices, 2 or 3 at a time, and cook each side for 3 to 4 minutes, or until fully cooked. Remove the eggplant from the skillet, and place on a plate lined with paper towel.

2. Repeat with the remaining eggplant slices. If the eggplant sticks, add a bit more olive oil to the skillet.

3. Layer the avocado, bacon, and arugula on top of the eggplant, and season with salt and pepper. Roll up the eggplant and secure with a toothpick.

SEASONAL SWAP: If eggplant is not in season, zucchini makes a great alternative and can usually be found year-round at your local market. Use a mandoline to make quick work of slicing the veggies.

PORTOBELLO PHILLY CHEESESTEAK

SERVES 2 • PREP TIME 5 minute • COOK TIME 30 minutes

*I'm sure the die-hard Philly Cheesesteak fans
will be shocked that I'm not using bread to
hold this decadent meat and cheese delight
together, but I promise they'll love what I've
done here. The portobello mushroom "bun"
adds a hearty earthiness to this classic and can
be prepared at home in almost no time at all.*

1 TABLESPOON OLIVE OIL

½ SWEET ONION, SLICED

1 GARLIC CLOVE, MINCED

SEA SALT

FRESHLY GROUND BLACK PEPPER

8 OUNCES THINLY SLICED ROAST BEEF

2 PORTOBELLO MUSHROOM CAPS, CLEANED AND
    TRIMMED WITH GILLS REMOVED

4 SLICES PROVOLONE CHEESE

1. Preheat the oven to 400°F.

2. In a nonstick pan, heat the olive oil
over medium heat. Add the onion and
sauté for 3 to 4 minutes. Add the garlic,
season with salt and pepper, and cook for
another minute.

3. Add the roast beef and cook for another
5 minutes. Remove from the heat.

4. Lightly coat the outside of the mushroom
caps with olive oil. Arrange the mushroom
caps face-up on a sheet pan lined with foil.

5. Place one slice of the provolone cheese in
each mushroom cap. Fill each cap with roast
beef mixture. Season with salt and pepper.

6. Carefully place the sheet pan into the
oven, and bake for 15 to 20 minutes, or until
the cheese is golden brown.

SEASONAL SWAP: If you can't find large enough
mushrooms at your local market, bell peppers
make a great alternative. Simply cut off the top
and remove the seeds first.

CLASSIC BURGER

SERVES 2 • PREP TIME 5 minute • COOK TIME 15 minutes

I call this recipe the "Classic Burger" because that's just what it is—a no-frills American classic that even a novice chef can master. The most important step in perfecting your burger is making sure that you flip it at the right time so you cook it only once on each side. Like this, you seal in the rich flavor of the meat's juices. Our favorite thing about "burger night" is that you can easily customize your meal with a variety of toppings and condiments.

½ POUND GROUND BEEF
SEA SALT
FRESHLY GROUND BLACK PEPPER
2 HAMBURGER BUNS
½ TOMATO, SLICED
¼ ONION, SLICED
2 LETTUCE LEAVES

Optional Add-ins
BACON, COOKED
CARAMELIZED ONION
AVOCADO, SLICED
PICKLES

1. Heat the grill or a grill pan on the stove over medium heat.

2. Form the ground beef into two patties, and season generously with salt and pepper.

3. Grill the patties for about 4 minutes on each side. The patties should be fully cooked and deep brown on the outside, and slightly pink on the inside.

4. Serve each patty on a hamburger bun and top with tomato, onion, and lettuce.

PAIR UP: If you are gluten-free you can use gluten-free hamburger buns. If you are grain-free, omit the buns and use lettuce to turn the burger into a wrap.

≫TIPS FOR SUCCESSFUL COOKING≪

My priority when cooking during the week is that each meal is quick and easy to make. That's why all the recipes in this book can be made with five ingredients in 30 minutes or less. I am also a firm believer in planning and prepping meals over the weekend to ensure a stress-free week. The following are my tips for maximizing efficiency in the kitchen and planning the week's meals.

KEEP IT ORGANIZED Keep frequently used ingredients and cooking tools within easy reach. Clean up as you go, and return things to their proper place so you always know where everything is.

PLAN AHEAD Take the guesswork out of your week by planning your meals in advance. Organize a week of meals over the weekend so that you don't need to agonize over what to make each night.

MAKE A LIST Once you have planned your meals for the week, make a list of all the ingredients you'll need to pick up. Take inventory of what you already have in the pantry, then go shopping for the groceries you still need.

STOCK UP While planning ahead will make your week go smoothly, it is also important to have a variety of ingredients on hand so that you can make a nourishing impromptu meal anytime. Be sure to stock up on nonperishable pantry staples, as well as a variety of fresh fruits and veggies every week.

PREP AHEAD When possible, cook all the grains you'll need for the week ahead of time and chop all your veggies in advance. Dedicate one day over the weekend to prepping, and refrigerate everything in airtight containers. Not only will this save you time during the week, it will also reduce dish-washing and cleanup time.

DOUBLE UP My favorite trick when prepping is to double the recipe. By making an extra serving (or two), you'll have enough for lunch the next day.

4

VEGETARIAN

Roasted Veggie Kabobs 58

Grilled Zucchini Tacos 59

Simple Sheet-Pan Veggies 60

Buddha Bowl 61

Sweet Potato Stuffed with
Spinach and Feta 62

Roasted Eggplant with Brussels
Sprouts Salad 63

Spaghetti Squash and Pesto 64

Mexican Brown Rice 65

Cauliflower Pizza 66

Mushroom Risotto 67

Butternut Squash Curry 68

Cheesy Polenta with Brussels
Sprouts and Mushrooms 69

Mushrooms Stuffed with
Cheese and Herbs 70

Sweet Potato Gnocchi 71

Simple Eggplant Lasagna 72

MUSHROOMS STUFFED WITH CHEESE AND HERBS (OPPOSITE), PAGE 70

ROASTED VEGGIE KABOBS

SERVES 2 • PREP TIME 15 minutes • COOK TIME 10 minutes

Growing up, I loved to help my mom thread skewers when we were grilling kabobs for a big family barbecue. I had so much fun making patterns with the colorful vegetables, but I always made a few special kabobs for myself that were filled with just meat—no veggies. It's hard to believe that I didn't like the bold flavors of those colorful vegetables. Now I can't get enough. Although kabobs do make a fun and easy addition to a summer barbecue, they are just as special as a weeknight dinner for two. If you don't love the suggested veggie combo, you can opt to leave out a veggie or simply replace it with your favorite. Summer squash, red onions, and zucchini work great, too.

½ TEASPOON GROUND CUMIN

½ TEASPOON SMOKED PAPRIKA

2 CUPS GRAPE TOMATOES

2 CUPS SMALL BROCCOLI FLORETS

1 CUP HALVED BUTTON MUSHROOMS

2 TABLESPOONS EXTRA-VIRGIN OLIVE OIL

SEA SALT

FRESHLY GROUND BLACK PEPPER

1. Heat the grill to medium heat. In a small bowl, combine the cumin and smoked paprika.

2. In a large bowl, combine the tomatoes, broccoli, mushrooms, and olive oil. Toss until evenly coated.

3. Thread the vegetables onto skewers, and sprinkle with the cumin and paprika.

4. Place on the grill and cook for 6 to 10 minutes, turning over once. Remove from the grill, transfer to a serving platter, cover with aluminum foil, and let cool for 5 minutes. Season with salt and pepper and serve.

DID YOU KNOW? Don't have a grill? Roast the veggies in the oven instead. Rather than threading them onto barbecue skewers, simply spread the veggies in a single layer on a sheet pan lined with foil, and roast at 475°F for 15 to 20 minutes.

GRILLED ZUCCHINI TACOS

SERVES 2 • PREP TIME 5 minutes • COOK TIME 5 minutes

My two favorite things about Boston are the people and the food. Luckily for us, we get to enjoy both when we double-date with friends. Across town from where we live, there is a cute little taquería and oyster bar that serves the tastiest street tacos and the strongest margaritas. So it's no surprise that it is our go-to spot when we go out with friends who live in that area. We crave these tacos more often than we visit the taquería, so I had to learn to re-create them at home. I hope you love them as much as we do!

1 TABLESPOON EXTRA-VIRGIN OLIVE OIL

2 ZUCCHINIS, CUT INTO 1-INCH STICKS

1 GARLIC CLOVE, MINCED

½ JALAPEÑO, SEEDS REMOVED AND MINCED

SEA SALT

FRESHLY GROUND BLACK PEPPER

4 SMALL CORN TORTILLAS

1 CUP SHREDDED RED CABBAGE

Optional Add-ins

FRESH CILANTRO

PICKLED RED ONION

LIME WEDGES

1. In a large cast-iron skillet, heat the olive oil over medium heat. Add the zucchini, garlic, and jalapeño and cook for 1 minute. Season with salt and pepper. Stir and cook for another minute, until the zucchini is crisp-tender and lightly browned. Pour the zucchini mixture into a bowl and wipe the skillet clean.

2. Reheat the skillet over high heat. Add the tortillas one at a time and heat for about 20 seconds on each side.

3. Assemble the tacos by spooning the zucchini on half the tortillas and fold over the ingredients. Top with the cabbage and add additional toppings as desired.

PAIR UP: For even more flavor and a bit of heat, toss the cabbage with chipotle mayo, lime juice, and a sprinkle of salt before topping the tacos.

SIMPLE SHEET-PAN VEGGIES

SERVES 2 • PREP TIME 10 minutes • COOK TIME 20 minutes

I used to avoid vegetables at all costs—until I learned how to roast them properly. Now I often opt for a bowl full of roasted veggies for dinner because it makes for an easy and nutrient-packed dinner. I personally love the combination of broccoli, carrots, mushrooms, and shallots, but this is a great recipe for incorporating leftover vegetables to create your own combination.

1 SMALL HEAD BROCCOLI, TRIMMED
    INTO FLORETS
8 CARROTS, STEMS REMOVED
6 OUNCES WHITE MUSHROOMS, HALVED
2 SHALLOTS, CUT INTO SIXTHS
1 TABLESPOON EXTRA-VIRGIN OLIVE OIL
2 GARLIC CLOVES, MINCED
SEA SALT
FRESHLY GROUND BLACK PEPPER

1. Preheat the oven to 425°F.

2. On a sheet pan lined with foil, arrange the broccoli, carrots, mushrooms, and shallots. Drizzle the veggies with the olive oil. Season with the garlic, salt, and pepper, and toss to coat evenly.

3. Place the vegetables into the oven and roast for 20 minutes, or until they are lightly browned.

BUDDHA BOWL

SERVES 2 • PREP TIME 5 minutes • COOK TIME 25 minutes

True to its name, this dish is so loaded with quinoa and veggies that the top of the bowl resembles a rounded Buddha belly. Much like a salad, there is no single version of this dish. This recipe calls for my favorite veggies, but you can swap these for whatever you have on hand. Love the idea of a Buddha Bowl but need more inspiration? My third cookbook, Clean Eating Bowls, *is packed with recipes that fit the bill.*

½ SWEET POTATO, CHOPPED

10 GREEN ASPARAGUS, ENDS TRIMMED

2 TABLESPOONS EXTRA-VIRGIN OLIVE OIL

½ CUP QUINOA, RINSED AND DRAINED

1 CUP WATER

½ CUP CANNED RED BEANS, DRAINED AND RINSED

1 AVOCADO, CHOPPED

1. Preheat the oven to 400°F.

2. On a sheet pan lined with aluminum foil, spread out the sweet potato and asparagus in a single layer, and drizzle with the olive oil. Place the sheet pan in the oven and bake for 20 to 25 minutes.

3. Meanwhile, in a large pot, add the quinoa and water and bring to a boil over high heat, stirring frequently. Reduce the heat to low and simmer for 15 to 20 minutes, stirring occasionally.

4. Once the water is absorbed and the quinoa is tender, remove the pot from the heat. Use a fork to fluff the quinoa, transfer it to a large bowl, and let cool.

5. Divide the quinoa into two bowls and top with the roasted veggies, beans, and avocado.

PAIR UP: While you don't necessarily need to dress a Buddha Bowl to make it delicious, I do love to add a drizzle of creamy tahini dressing for a boost of flavor. Try whisking together 4 tablespoons of tahini, 2 tablespoons of lemon juice, 1 tablespoon of tamari, and a splash of water to give your bowl even more flavor.

SWEET POTATO STUFFED *with* SPINACH *and* FETA

SERVES 2 • PREP TIME 10 minutes • COOK TIME 10 minutes

When I lived alone, a baked sweet potato was a quick and easy "meal" that I would make on busy weeknights. Sometimes I would add leftover chicken or toss black beans and ground beef on top, but most of the time I just added a little butter and a sprinkle of cinnamon. When I moved in with Julien, I wanted to step up my sweet potato game, so I came up with this Mediterranean-inspired dish. The microwave method outlined in the recipe is the fastest way to get a meal on the table, but if you have more time you can also roast the sweet potatoes in the oven for an hour at 400°F.

2 SWEET POTATOES

1 TABLESPOON EXTRA-VIRGIN OLIVE OIL

2 GARLIC CLOVE, MINCED

3 CUPS THINLY SLICED SPINACH

2 TABLESPOONS HUMMUS

4 TABLESPOONS FETA CHEESE

FRESHLY GROUND BLACK PEPPER

1. Pierce the sweet potatoes several times with a fork. Place them on a paper towel in the microwave and cook each side for 3 to 4 minutes, or until tender. Remove from the microwave and let them cool for several minutes.

2. Cut each sweet potato in half lengthwise and scoop out the flesh. Set the skins aside. Place the flesh in a large bowl and mash it with a fork.

3. In a medium cast-iron skillet, heat the olive oil over medium heat. Add the garlic and sauté until browned. Add the spinach and cook until the spinach is wilted, about 1 minute, stirring occasionally.

4. Add the spinach mixture to the bowl with the mashed sweet potato. Add the hummus and feta cheese. Stir gently to combine. Season with pepper.

5. Fill the sweet potato skins with the sweet potato and spinach mixture.

SEASONAL SWAP: If you're craving a more comforting dish in the colder months, try swapping these Mediterranean flavors for maple syrup, cinnamon, and chopped pecans.

ROASTED EGGPLANT *with* BRUSSELS SPROUTS SALAD

SERVES 2 • PREP TIME 5 minutes • COOK TIME 30 minutes

I used to be completely intimidated by eggplant, but the truth is that it's super versatile and easy to prepare in a variety of ways—plus it pairs well with a wide range of flavors. The thick flesh is hearty enough to take center stage, and makes a great meat replacement. This recipe is perfect if you are new to cooking eggplant. All you need to do is roast the eggplant until the skin looks collapsed and puckered. Because it is so simple and delicious, this is sure to make it into your weeknight dinner rotation.

2 SMALL EGGPLANTS, STEMS REMOVED
    AND HALVED
4 TABLESPOONS EXTRA-VIRGIN OLIVE
    OIL, DIVIDED
½ TEASPOON SMOKED PAPRIKA
SEA SALT
FRESHLY GROUND BLACK PEPPER
2 QUARTS WATER
1 CUP THINLY SLICED BRUSSELS SPROUTS,
    ENDS TRIMMED
JUICE OF 1 LEMON
1 TABLESPOON HONEY

Optional Add-in
FRESH PARSLEY, CHOPPED, FOR GARNISH

1. Preheat the oven to 400°F.

2. Lightly coat the eggplant with the olive oil and season with the paprika, salt, and pepper. Place it face-down on a sheet pan lined with aluminum foil, and roast for 25 to 30 minutes, or until the eggplant skin looks collapsed.

3. Meanwhile, in a large pot over high heat, bring the water to a boil. Add the Brussels sprouts and blanch them for 1 minute. Remove from the heat, pour through a colander, and rinse immediately with cold water. Drain well.

4. In a small bowl, whisk the remaining olive oil, lemon juice, and honey.

5. In a large bowl, combine the Brussels sprouts and dressing. Toss to coat evenly.

6. When the eggplants are completely baked through, remove them from the oven. Top with the Brussels sprout salad and serve.

DID YOU KNOW? Although it is usually available year-round, eggplant is at its peak from July to October. When selecting eggplant at the market, look for those with firm, glossy skin.

SPAGHETTI SQUASH *and* PESTO

SERVES 2 • PREP TIME 5 minutes • COOK TIME 30 minutes

When Julien and I took our first trip to Italy, we visited the Liguria region, which is cited as the pesto capital of the world. During our trip we had pesto on everything and anything we could get our hands on—from pasta and pizza to Italian chickpea pancakes called farinata. *We were never disappointed. Our trip not only solidified our love for all things pesto, it also inspired the location for our upcoming wedding. Now, whenever we are making pesto at home, it reminds us of that first international trip together and brings back some of our best memories.*

1 SMALL SPAGHETTI SQUASH

½ CUP PINE NUTS

3 CUPS PACKED FRESH BASIL

3 GARLIC CLOVES, ROUGHLY CHOPPED

1 TEASPOON SEA SALT

½ CUP EXTRA-VIRGIN OLIVE OIL

⅓ CUP FINELY GRATED PARMESAN CHEESE

1. Cut the spaghetti squash in half lengthwise. Using a large spoon, scrape out all the seeds from each half. Place the squash face-down on a microwave-safe plate and microwave on high for 15 minutes, or until the squash is soft.

2. While the squash is cooking, preheat the oven to 375°F. Lay the pine nuts on a sheet pan lined with parchment paper. Roast for 8 minutes. Remove from the oven and set aside to cool.

3. In a food processor, combine the pine nuts, basil, garlic, and sea salt. With the food processor running, slowly add the olive oil until the ingredients are fully combined. Add the Parmesan and pulse to combine.

4. Remove the squash from the microwave, and turn the halves over so they are face-up. Allow the squash to cool for 5 minutes. Scrape the insides of the squash halves with a large fork to create "spaghetti" strands.

5. In a large bowl, combine the spaghetti squash and pesto. Toss to coat evenly and serve.

PAIR UP: I love using spaghetti squash instead of pasta because it is an easy way to sneak in more vegetables, but feel free to swap squash for your favorite pasta if you are not grain-free.

MEXICAN BROWN RICE

SERVES 2 • PREP TIME 5 minutes • COOK TIME 10 minutes

Meatless Monday doesn't have to be boring. This Mexican-inspired spin on a traditional fried rice dish is full of flavor and ready in minutes! I like to use leftover brown rice because it crisps up well in the skillet, but you can use whatever grain you have on hand. Leftover quinoa from your Sunday meal prep works great too!

1 CUP BROWN RICE

1 TABLESPOON EXTRA-VIRGIN OLIVE OIL

½ CUP FROZEN CORN KERNELS

1 (15-OUNCE) CAN BLACK BEANS, DRAINED
    AND RINSED

½ TABLESPOON GROUND CUMIN

½ CUP FRESH SALSA

Optional Add-in
FRESH CILANTRO, FOR GARNISH

1. Prepare the rice according to its package. Set aside.

2. In a medium cast-iron skillet, heat the olive oil over medium heat. Add the corn and black beans, and cook for 2 to 3 minutes, or until the corn is tender.

3. Add the rice and cumin to the skillet and stir to combine. Cook for 2 to 3 minutes, or until the rice begins to crisp. Stir in the salsa and cook for another 2 to 3 minutes.

4. Remove the skillet from the heat and let cool for 5 minutes, fluff the rice with a fork, and serve.

CAULIFLOWER PIZZA

SERVES 2 • PREP TIME 5 minutes • COOK TIME 25 minutes

The first time Julien and I made cauliflower pizza was in our first apartment. I remember grating the cauliflower by hand at the coffee table because we didn't have a food processor, and because there was not enough space for the both of us in the kitchen. Although the cauliflower pizza crust was delicious, it took too long to cook and crumbled once we finally dug in. I vowed to never spend that much time making pizza again. Well, after a little trial and error, I've finally mastered the art of the cauliflower pizza. This version holds together no matter what toppings you throw on it, and it's ready in under 30 minutes!

1 HEAD CAULIFLOWER, STEM REMOVED

¼ CUP GRATED PARMESAN CHEESE

¼ TEASPOON SEA SALT

1 EGG

2 CUPS GRATED FRESH MOZZARELLA CHEESE

¼ CUP MARINARA SAUCE

Optional Add-in
FRESH BASIL LEAVES

1. Preheat the oven to 425°F.

2. Cut the cauliflower into florets. Place the florets into a food processor and pulse until the cauliflower is a very fine consistency.

3. Place the riced cauliflower into a microwave-safe bowl and microwave for 4 to 6 minutes, or until soft. Transfer the cauliflower onto a kitchen towel and let it cool. Using the towel, soak up as much moisture as possible from the cauliflower.

4. In a large bowl, add the cauliflower, Parmesan cheese, sea salt, egg, and 1 cup of mozzarella cheese. Mix until well combined. Transfer the cauliflower mixture to a sheet pan lined with parchment paper, and flatten it into a 10-inch disk. Bake for 10 to 15 minutes, or until golden brown.

5. Top the crust with the marinara sauce and the remaining 1 cup of mozzarella cheese. Bake for another 8 to 10 minutes, until the cheese is melted and bubbly.

PAIR UP: Pile on the veggies to really take this pizza to the next level. Add onions, peppers, and anything else you love on a traditional pizza.

MUSHROOM RISOTTO

SERVES 2 • PREP TIME 5 minutes • COOK TIME 25 minutes

Few dishes are as exquisite as a rich, creamy risotto. This is my favorite recipe for a special occasion because it is decadent and delicious, without being overly complicated. I think some people stay away from making risotto at home because it sounds like a long, laborious process, but this version takes just five ingredients and 30 minutes. In the spring, you can replace the mushrooms with fresh asparagus, peas, and fiddleheads for a different seasonal take.

2 TABLESPOONS BUTTER, DIVIDED

2 GARLIC CLOVES, MINCED, DIVIDED

1 CUP ARBORIO RICE

2 CUPS VEGETABLE BROTH

6 OUNCES BABY BELLA MUSHROOMS, SLICED

SEA SALT

FRESHLY GROUND BLACK PEPPER

Optional Add-ins

¼ CUP PARMESAN CHEESE, FOR GARNISH

1. In a medium nonstick pan, heat 1 tablespoon of the butter over medium heat. Add 1 garlic clove and sauté for about 1 minute.

2. Add the Arborio rice and mix with the butter and garlic. Add 1 cup of vegetable broth and stir continuously. When most of the broth has evaporated, add another ½ cup and stir continuously. Keep stirring for 15 minutes, or until the rice is cooked and the mixture begins to get creamy. If necessary, add the remaining broth in small batches to ensure that the rice is fully cooked.

3. In a separate pan, heat the remaining butter over medium heat. Add the remaining garlic clove and sauté for another minute. Add the mushrooms and sauté for 5 minutes, or until browned.

4. Remove the mushrooms from the heat and transfer to the risotto pan. Season with salt and pepper.

BUTTERNUT SQUASH CURRY

SERVES 2 • PREP TIME 10 minutes • COOK TIME 20 minutes

Okay, I'm going to admit something here: This curry recipe is not exactly "authentic." I don't use all of the fancy spices, so the dish will not taste exactly like the curry dish from your favorite Indian restaurant. But I promise that you will find this recipe absolutely lick-the-bowl delicious, not to mention quick and easy! Just five ingredients and 30 minutes stands between you and this yummy takeout-inspired meal for two.

1 TABLESPOON EXTRA-VIRGIN OLIVE OIL

1 TABLESPOON MINCED FRESH GINGER

1 TABLESPOON RED CURRY PASTE

½ CUP FULL-FAT COCONUT MILK

¼ CUP WATER

2 CUPS CUBED BUTTERNUT SQUASH

1 (15-OUNCE) CAN FIRE-ROASTED
    DICED TOMATOES

SEA SALT

Optional Add-ins

BROWN RICE, FOR SERVING

FRESH CILANTRO, FOR GARNISH

1. In a medium cast-iron skillet, heat the olive oil over medium heat. Add the ginger and sauté for 1 minute. Stir in the curry paste and cook until the paste becomes fragrant.

2. Add the coconut milk and water, and stir until well combined. Add the butternut squash and tomatoes; toss to coat evenly.

3. Bring the mixture to a simmer, cover, and cook for 10 to 15 minutes, or until the squash is tender. Remove from the heat, season with salt, and let stand for 5 minutes.

PAIR UP: If you prefer a thicker curry sauce, simply whisk in ½ tablespoon of tapioca flour or cornstarch before removing from the heat.

CHEESY POLENTA *with* BRUSSELS SPROUTS *and* MUSHROOMS

SERVES 2 • PREP TIME 10 minutes • COOK TIME 20 minutes

When I dine out, I love to order a bunch of small plates so that I can try a variety of dishes. There is one restaurant in particular where I always opt for two or three sides instead of an entrée. The waiters are usually puzzled at first, but after I've ordered they often tell me I've chosen some of their favorites! Since Julien and I don't have the time (or the finances) to dine out every night, I turned my favorite side dishes into a meal that is sure to delight. Here, creamy and cheesy polenta, crispy Brussels sprouts, and earthy mushrooms all come together for a dish that is as delicious as it is comforting.

1 CUP QUARTERED BRUSSELS SPROUTS, ENDS TRIMMED
1 CUP SLICED WILD MUSHROOMS
1 TABLESPOON EXTRA-VIRGIN OLIVE OIL
SEA SALT
FRESHLY GROUND BLACK PEPPER
2 CUPS WATER
½ CUP INSTANT POLENTA
2 TABLESPOONS CHOPPED FRESH SAGE
½ CUP PARMESAN CHEESE, DIVIDED

1. Preheat the oven to 400°F.

2. In a large bowl, combine the Brussels sprouts, mushrooms, and olive oil. Toss to evenly coat, and season with salt and pepper. Transfer to a sheet pan lined with parchment paper, and bake for 15 to 20 minutes, or until lightly browned.

3. Meanwhile, in a large pot, bring the water to a boil. Reduce the heat to low and slowly whisk in the polenta. Continue to whisk until the polenta has thickened, about 3 minutes.

4. Remove from the heat and stir in the sage and ¼ cup of the Parmesan cheese. Season with salt and pepper.

5. Divide the polenta between 2 bowls, and top each one with the Brussels sprouts and mushrooms, and then sprinkle with the remaining Parmesan cheese.

MUSHROOMS STUFFED *with* CHEESE *and* HERBS

SERVES 2 • PREP TIME 5 minutes • COOK TIME 25 minutes

Julien is a sucker for two things: goat cheese and mushrooms. So I knew he'd go nuts for this dish. It has all the gooey goodness of melted goat cheese, flavored with fresh herbs and stuffed into a portobello mushroom cap. Portobello mushrooms are hearty and satisfying, but if you're feeling extra hungry, you can just double the recipe!

2 PORTOBELLO MUSHROOMS

1 TABLESPOON EXTRA-VIRGIN OLIVE OIL

8 OUNCES GOAT CHEESE, CRUMBLED

2 SLICES OF BREAD

½ CUP FRESH PARSLEY, CHOPPED

1 GARLIC CLOVE, MINCED

SEA SALT

FRESHLY GROUND BLACK PEPPER

Optional Add-ins

CRUSHED RED PEPPER FLAKES, FOR GARNISH

1. Preheat the oven to 425°F.

2. Lightly coat the outside of the mushroom caps with the olive oil. Arrange the mushroom caps face-up on a sheet pan lined with parchment paper.

3. In a food processor, combine goat cheese, bread, and parsley. Pulse until combined.

4. Fill each mushroom cap with the goat cheese mixture. Sprinkle with the minced garlic and season with salt and pepper.

5. Carefully place the sheet pan into the oven and bake for 15 to 20 minutes, or until the cheese is melted and lightly brown.

PAIR UP: Elevate this dish by adding fresh crab or lobster to the filling.

SWEET POTATO GNOCCHI

SERVES 2 • PREP TIME 20 minutes • COOK TIME 10 minutes

Don't skip over this recipe because you think that homemade pasta sounds tedious and time consuming. This recipe is just the opposite! In just 30 minutes and with just five ingredients, you will be a gnocchi master before you know it. This recipe is also a great opportunity for you and your significant other to cook together! If you prefer russet potatoes, they can easily be used instead of sweet potato. I like to sprinkle a little olive oil and fresh herbs on my gnocchi, but you can also top this dish with your favorite marinara, Alfredo, or pesto sauce if you prefer.

¼ CUP MILLET FLOUR

¼ CUP PLUS 1 TABLESPOON ALMOND FLOUR

¼ CUP PLUS 1 TABLESPOON TAPIOCA STARCH

¼ TEASPOON SALT

½ CUP PLUS 2 TABLESPOONS ROASTED AND
    MASHED SWEET POTATO

2 QUARTS WATER

1 TABLESPOON EXTRA-VIRGIN OLIVE OIL

1. In a small bowl, combine the millet flour, almond flour, tapioca starch, and salt.

2. In a large bowl, combine the mashed sweet potato and half of the flour mixture. Knead with your hands. Add the remaining half of the flour mixture and continue to knead the dough into a ball.

3. Lightly dust a clean work surface with flour and flatten the dough into a round disk. Divide the disk into four pieces. Roll out one of the piece, into a 6-inch-long pipe, about ½ inch wide. Cut this pipe into 1-inch-long pieces, and press down gently on the top of each piece with the tines of a fork to make the individual gnocchi.

4. Repeat for the remaining pieces of dough. Be sure to lightly coat the surface with flour each time so that it doesn't stick.

5. In a large pot, add the water and bring to a boil over high heat. Add half of the gnocchi and cook for 2 minutes. When they begin to float, remove the gnocchi from the water with a slotted spoon and set aside. Repeat with the remaining dough. When all the gnocchi are cooked, place them the refrigerator for 5 minutes.

6. In a medium nonstick pan, heat the olive oil over medium heat. Sauté the gnocchi for 5 to 6 minutes, stirring frequently, until they are crispy on the outside. Sprinkle with salt and serve.

SIMPLE EGGPLANT LASAGNA

SERVES 2 • PREP TIME 5 minutes • COOK TIME 30 minutes

This vegetarian dish has all the cheesy, saucy goodness you'd expect from lasagna, but without the heaviness of pasta. Instead, thinly sliced eggplant takes center stage. So when you and your significant other are craving a comforting meal, this lasagna is sure to fit the bill.

1 LARGE EGGPLANT, SLICED ABOUT ½-INCH THICK

1 TABLESPOON EXTRA-VIRGIN OLIVE OIL

1 TEASPOON GARLIC POWDER

1 TEASPOON ITALIAN SEASONING

¼ CUP MARINARA SAUCE

¼ CUP GRATED MOZZARELLA CHEESE

1. Preheat the oven to 400°F.

2. Lightly coat the eggplant with the olive oil, and season with the garlic powder and Italian seasoning. Spread the slices in a single layer on a sheet pan lined with aluminum foil.

3. Roast the eggplant for 10 minutes, flip it, and roast for another 5 to 10 minutes, or until it is soft and lightly browned.

4. In a small baking dish, layer the eggplant, marinara sauce, and mozzarella cheese. Repeat this layering with the remaining ingredients.

5. Cover the baking dish with foil and bake for 5 to 8 minutes, or until the cheese is hot and bubbly. Uncover and bake until the cheese is lightly browned.

DID YOU KNOW? During a busy week, sometimes even five minutes feels like too much time spent prepping a meal. Luckily you can prep this one in advance—just assemble the lasagna over the weekend so you can easily pop it in the oven when you get home from work.

❧SHOP SMART❧

These days, it seems as if we are constantly being told that more is better. With grocery store aisles full of buy-one-get-one-free sale items and better deals for bigger quantities, it is particularly challenging for smaller households to buy exactly what they need without overspending or overbuying. The following are my tips for buying foods in smaller quantities and for dealing with bulk items.

BUY ONLY WHAT YOU NEED When shopping, stick to your grocery list and buy only what you really need. Don't feel pressured by sale items and family-sized packaging— you will just end up wasting money by having to throw away excess products if you don't use them in time. In the produce aisle, get specific with how much of each product you'll need for the week.

SHOP AT THE MEAT COUNTER Most of the recipes in this book call for less than one pound of meat, yet beef, chicken, and pork are often prepackaged in increments of one pound or more. Don't feel forced to buy more than you need. Instead, head over to the meat counter and ask the butcher for the exact amount.

FILL YOUR FREEZER While I prefer fresh fruits and vegetables, I always have a few bags of frozen produce in the freezer. I buy frozen fruit and berries such as mango, pineapple, strawberries, blueberries, and raspberries in bulk so I can add them to my desserts year-round. I also buy frozen veggies like broccoli, cauliflower, corn, and peas because they are easy to toss into a skillet or roast in the oven.

BUY BULK FOODS Just don't buy them in bulk. The bulk food aisle allows you to purchase dry goods like grains, beans, nuts, and spices in the exact quantity you need, big or small.

5

SEAFOOD

Orange Shrimp with Green Beans en Papillote 76

Grilled Halibut and Rice 77

Roasted Honey-Garlic Salmon 78

Lemon Risotto and Shrimp 79

Mediterranean Baked Salmon 80

Simple Shrimp Scampi 81

Prosciutto-Wrapped Scallops 82

Pan-Seared Scallops in a White Wine Sauce 83

Sheet-Pan Salmon with Mushrooms and Peppers 84

Mussels and Chorizo in Red Wine Sauce 85

ROASTED HONEY-GARLIC SALMON (OPPOSITE), PAGE 78

ORANGE SHRIMP *with* GREEN BEANS EN PAPILLOTE

SERVES 2 • PREP TIME 15 minutes • COOK TIME 15 minutes

"En papillote" may sound like a super fancy French cooking technique, but the truth is that cooking in parchment locks in flavor without much effort. Not to mention that cleanup is a breeze! Simply arrange a few ingredients on the parchment, fold it up, and the paper does all the work locking in flavor and moisture. When cooking for two, you can make either two separate parchment packets or one big one if you have big enough parchment paper.

8 OUNCES GREEN BEANS, ENDS TRIMMED

SEA SALT

12 EXTRA-LARGE SHRIMP, PEELED AND DEVEINED

FRESHLY GROUND BLACK PEPPER

1 ORANGE, PEELED, PITH REMOVED, AND
    SEGMENTED

1 TEASPOON MINCED FRESH GINGER

¼ CUP DRY WHITE WINE

Optional Add-ins

3 CARROTS, PEELED, TRIMMED, AND CUT
    INTO MATCHSTICKS

2 FRESH THYME SPRIGS

1. Preheat the oven to 400°F. Place a large sheet pan in the oven to preheat.

2. Fold two 14-by-12-inch pieces of parchment paper in half. Using kitchen shears, cut the folded paper into a half-heart shape, then unfold it so it is in the shape of a full heart.

3. Arrange the green beans tightly together on one side of each paper heart. Season with salt. Place the shrimp on top of the green beans and season with pepper.

4. Arrange the orange slices on top of the shrimp and sprinkle with the ginger. Drizzle the wine on top. Be sure to keep the wine on top of the shrimp and veggies.

5. Working from one end, tightly fold the open edge of the paper to form a seal.

6. Transfer the packet to the preheated sheet pan. Bake for 12 minutes. Remove from the oven and let cool for 3 minutes.

7. Carefully open the paper packets, being careful of the steam, and serve.

GRILLED HALIBUT *and* RICE

SERVES 2 • PREP TIME 15 minutes • COOK TIME 10 minutes

The technique used here is similar to that used in the recipe for Orange Shrimp with Green Beans en Papillote (see page 76), but we use aluminum foil instead of parchment paper to contain the flavor. I love this technique because it makes grilling fish simple and less intimidating. Just make sure to double the aluminum foil to ensure that the rice on the bottom does not burn.

1 CUP WATER, PLUS 1 TABLESPOON

1 CUP INSTANT BROWN RICE

1 TABLESPOON ORANGE JUICE

½ TABLESPOON MINCED FRESH GINGER

½ TABLESPOON TOASTED SESAME OIL

COCONUT OIL

½ POUND SKINLESS HALIBUT FILLET, HALVED

1. Preheat the grill.

2. In a small pot over medium heat, bring 1 cup of water to a simmer. Add the rice and set aside, uncovered, for 10 minutes. In a small bowl, add the orange juice, ginger, sesame oil, and the remaining water. Whisk until well combined.

3. On a work surface, layer two 20-inch pieces of aluminum foil. Lightly grease the top layer with coconut oil. Place ½ cup of the rice in the middle of the foil. Top the rice with a piece of fish, and drizzle with half of the orange juice mixture.

4. Bring the short ends of the foil together. Working from one end, tightly fold over the open edge of the paper to form a seal. Make another foil packet with the remaining ingredients.

5. Place the packets on the preheated grill and cook for 8 to 12 minutes, or until the fish is opaque in the center. Remove from the grill.

6. Carefully open the foil packets, letting the steam escape, and serve.

EQUIPMENT TIP: If you do not have a grill, you can replicate this technique in the oven by replacing the aluminum foil with parchment paper and cooking at 400°F.

ROASTED HONEY-GARLIC SALMON

SERVES 2 • PREP TIME 5 minutes • COOK TIME 10 minutes

This is a wonderfully easy dish that takes 15 minutes from start to finish. Don't be intimated by the prospect of cooking fish at home—this foolproof beginner recipe is simple but still filled with flavor. I love how crispy the salmon skin gets in this recipe, but you can remove the skin if you prefer. Serve the salmon on top of brown rice and sautéed spinach, or with a side of your favorite vegetables.

4 TABLESPOONS HONEY

2 TABLESPOONS TAMARI

2 TEASPOONS WHITE VINEGAR

2 TABLESPOONS MINCED GARLIC CLOVES

2 (6-OUNCE) SALMON FILLETS, SKIN ON

SEA SALT

FRESHLY GROUND BLACK PEPPER

1 TABLESPOON EXTRA-VIRGIN OLIVE OIL

Optional Add-ins

BROWN RICE, FOR SERVING

SAUTÉED SPINACH, FOR SERVING

1. In a small bowl, whisk together the honey, tamari, vinegar, and garlic.

2. Pat the salmon dry with a paper towel, and season generously with salt and pepper.

3. In a large cast-iron skillet, heat the olive oil over high heat. Add the salmon, skin-side down, and immediately reduce the heat to medium. Press down gently to ensure that the skin cooks evenly. Cook for 5 to 8 minutes, or until it reaches desired doneness.

4. Drizzle about 1 tablespoon of the honey mixture on each fillet. Flip and cook the other side for 1 minute.

5. Remove the salmon from the skillet, and allow it to rest skin-side up for 3 minutes. Drizzle with the remaining honey mixture and serve.

DID YOU KNOW? You can determine how cooked the salmon is by looking at the side of the filet. For rare doneness, the middle should still be a bright coral color; if you want medium, remove it from the skillet when it just starts to darken. Alternatively, you can use a thermometer in the thickest part. It should be 120°F for rare or 130°F for medium.

LEMON RISOTTO *and* SHRIMP

SERVES 2 • PREP TIME 5 minutes • COOK TIME 25 minutes

If Mushroom Risotto (see page 67) is my favorite version of the Italian classic, then this is Julien's. It's incredible how much flavor a few simple ingredients can add. The risotto is rich and creamy without being too heavy, making it the perfect base for grilled shrimp, pan-seared scallops, or your favorite fish. If you prefer veggies, substitute the fish with peas and leeks and a sprinkle of fresh tarragon.

12 MEDIUM SHRIMP, PEELED AND DEVEINED
SEA SALT
FRESHLY GROUND BLACK PEPPER
2 TABLESPOONS FRESHLY SQUEEZED LEMON JUICE
1 TEASPOON OF LEMON ZEST
3 TABLESPOONS EXTRA-VIRGIN OLIVE OIL, DIVIDED
1 CLOVE GARLIC, MINCED AND DIVIDED
1 CUP ARBORIO RICE
2 CUPS VEGETABLE BROTH

Optional Add-ins
¼ CUP PARMESAN CHEESE
FRESH PARSLEY, FOR GARNISH

1. Preheat a grill pan over medium heat. Meanwhile, season both sides of the shrimp evenly with the salt, pepper, and olive oil.

2. Once the grill pan is hot, cook the shrimp for 3 minutes per side. Set aside, but cover with aluminum foil to keep warm.

3. In a medium nonstick pan, heat 1 tablespoon of olive oil over medium heat. Add the minced garlic and sauté for about 1 minute.

4. Add the Arborio rice and mix it with the olive oil and garlic. Add 1 cup of vegetable broth, lemon juice, and lemon zest, and stir continuously. When most of the broth has evaporated, add another ½ cup. Repeat for about 15 minutes, or until the Arborio rice has fully cooked and the mixture begins to get creamy. If necessary, add the remaining broth in small batches to ensure that the rice is fully cooked.

5. Remove the rice from the heat, and stir in the olive oil. Season with salt and pepper. Transfer the risotto to a serving dish, and top with the shrimp.

MEDITERRANEAN BAKED SALMON

SERVES 2 • PREP TIME 5 minutes • COOK TIME 10 minutes

If you haven't cooked fish before, this is the perfect place to start. And if you've been cooking fish for years, this recipe will still be perfect for you. While baked salmon is delicious on its own with just a pinch of salt and pepper, pairing it with just a few extra ingredients can take the dish to another level. In this recipe, we create a simple garlic-cilantro sauce that adds just enough flavor without taking away from the salmon itself. For easy cleanup, be sure to line the sheet pan with aluminum foil before lightly greasing it with oil.

4 GARLIC CLOVES

1 CUP FRESH CILANTRO, STEMS TRIMMED

¼ CUP EXTRA-VIRGIN OLIVE OIL

1 LEMON, HALVED

SEA SALT

FRESHLY GROUND BLACK PEPPER

1 POUND SKINLESS SALMON FILLET

½ TOMATO, SLICED INTO ROUNDS

1. Preheat the oven to 425°F.

2. In a small food processor, add the garlic, cilantro, olive oil, and juice from 1 lemon half. Season with salt, and blend until well combined.

3. On a lightly greased sheet pan, center the salmon fillet and sprinkle with salt and pepper. Spoon the garlic and cilantro sauce on top and spread to coat evenly. Cut the remaining lemon half into thin, round slices. Arrange the lemon and tomato slices on top of the salmon.

4. Bake for 10 to 12 minutes. Remove from the oven and cover with foil. Let sit for 8 minutes to finish cooking.

DID YOU KNOW? The most important rule when cooking salmon is to not overcook it. For perfectly flaky and tender salmon, all it takes is 4 to 6 minutes per ½ inch. Be sure to adjust the cook time as needed so that you get the best outcome every time.

SIMPLE SHRIMP SCAMPI

SERVES 2 • PREP TIME 10 minutes • COOK TIME 10 minutes

All the recipes in this book are meant to be simple and delicious, and this recipe is no exception. In fact, this scampi may be not only the most tried and true recipe in the book, but also the one with the fewest steps! Julien and I have been cooking a version of this recipe for as long as I can remember. Sometimes we switch up the veggies and use carrots or yellow squash in place of zucchini. Other times we switch out the shrimp for chicken. No matter how you make customize this recipe to your taste, it is sure to be a favorite.

2 TABLESPOONS BUTTER

5 GARLIC CLOVES, MINCED

2 ZUCCHINIS, SPIRALIZED INTO SPAGHETTI
    NOODLES

12 EXTRA-LARGE SHRIMP, PEELED AND DEVEINED

FRESHLY GROUND BLACK PEPPER

1. In a large cast-iron skillet over medium heat, melt the butter. Add the garlic and sauté for 1 to 2 minutes, or until lightly browned.

2. Turn the heat up to high, and add the zucchini and shrimp. Using metal tongs, toss the zucchini and shrimp for about 4 to 5 minutes, or until the shrimp is fully cooked. Season with pepper.

INGREDIENT SWAP: If you are not grain-free, you can use whole-wheat spaghetti instead of zucchini noodles if you prefer.

PROSCIUTTO-WRAPPED SCALLOPS

SERVES 2 • PREP TIME 15 minutes • COOK TIME 10 minutes

My favorite quick and easy appetizer for a dinner party or potluck is bacon-wrapped scallops. They are easy to pull together and everyone loves them. Who says you can't turn your favorite appetizer into a meal?! Here I've traded out the bacon for Italian prosciutto, which adds a more delicate and exquisite flavor. Serve over a bed of spinach, and you've turned this treat into a complete meal.

8 LARGE DRY SEA SCALLOPS

¼ TEASPOON LEMON PEPPER

1 OUNCE THINLY SLICED PROSCIUTTO, CUT INTO
    8 STRIPS

2 TABLESPOONS EXTRA-VIRGIN OLIVE OIL

1 TABLESPOON FRESHLY SQUEEZED LEMON JUICE

SEA SALT

FRESHLY GROUND BLACK PEPPER

8 OUNCES BABY SPINACH

1. Place the oven rack in the upper third of oven and preheat the broiler.

2. Pat the scallops dry and sprinkle with the lemon pepper. Wrap 1 strip of prosciutto around each scallop. Thread 4 scallops onto each skewer to secure the prosciutto.

3. Place the skewers on a lightly greased sheet pan lined with aluminum foil. Broil for 5 to 6 minutes, or until cooked to desired doneness.

4. In a small bowl, whisk together the olive oil and lemon juice. Season with salt and pepper and set aside.

5. Using a colander, rinse the spinach under cold water.

6. Heat a large cast-iron skillet over medium heat. Add the spinach and cook for 2 to 3 minutes, or until wilted. Drain the spinach if needed, and combine it with half of the oil and lemon mixture, tossing to coat.

7. Divide the spinach between two plates, and top each portion with 4 scallops. Drizzle the scallops with the remaining oil and lemon mixture.

PAIR UP: If you are unable to find thinly sliced prosciutto at your local market, you can simply use bacon.

PAN-SEARED SCALLOPS *in* A WHITE WINE SAUCE

SERVES 2 • PREP TIME 5 minutes • COOK TIME 15 minutes

Scallops were once thought of as a delicacy reserved for fancy restaurants. This reputation intimidates many people from trying to cook them at home, and their high cost makes experimentation a pricey endeavor. But the truth is that scallops are one of the easiest dishes to make at home. Pair them with a savory butter and white wine sauce, and you won't be able to tell the difference between your homemade version and the version at your favorite restaurant.

1 TABLESPOON EXTRA-VIRGIN OLIVE OIL

8 LARGE SEA SCALLOPS

⅓ CUP WHITE WINE

1 TABLESPOON WHITE ONION, MINCED

3 TABLESPOONS BUTTER

1½ TABLESPOONS FRESH PARSLEY, CHOPPED

SEA SALT

FRESHLY GROUND BLACK PEPPER

1. Preheat the oven to 150°F.

2. In a large nonstick pan, heat the olive oil over medium-high heat. When the pan is heated and the oil begins to smoke, add the scallops.

3. Sear until browned, flip, and cook for another 2 to 3 minutes. Remove the scallops from the pan, place them in an oven-safe plate or baking dish, and keep them warm in the oven.

4. Add the wine to the pan to deglaze it. Use a wooden spoon to scrape away the brown bits. Add the onion, and bring the wine to a boil. Boil until the liquid reduces to about 2 tablespoons, about 5 minutes.

5. Reduce the heat to low and stir in the butter, 1 tablespoon at a time, until fully incorporated. Season with the parsley, salt, and pepper. Douse the scallops with the sauce and serve.

DID YOU KNOW? When cooking the scallops, make sure the pan is nice and hot before adding the scallops. As soon as the scallops hit the pan, do not touch them or move them around.

SHEET-PAN SALMON *with* MUSHROOMS *and* PEPPERS

SERVES 2 • PREP TIME 15 minutes • COOK TIME 20 minutes

I am overjoyed that I have turned my passion for cooking into a career. Yet while outsiders might think that my life is glamorous and full of nightly gourmet dinners, the truth is that working full time, running a blog, and writing cookbooks is quite time consuming. I'm usually too drained to think about planning dinner, let alone cook it. That is why sheet-pan dishes like this one have become our go-to dinner during the week. Simply pile on your protein and veggies, add a simple sauce, and let the oven do all the work.

4 TABLESPOON MAPLE SYRUP

2 TABLESPOONS TAMARI

2 TEASPOON COCONUT OIL

¼ TEASPOON FRESHLY GROUND BLACK PEPPER

2 (6-OUNCE) SALMON FILLETS, SKIN INTACT

1 RED BELL PEPPER, SLICED AND SEEDS REMOVED

1 CUP SLICED SHIITAKE MUSHROOMS

Optional Add-ins

¼ CUP CHOPPED SCALLIONS, FOR GARNISH

TOASTED SESAME SEEDS, FOR GARNISH

JASMINE RICE, FOR SERVING

1. Preheat the oven to 475°F.

2. In a small bowl, whisk together the maple syrup, tamari, coconut oil, and pepper.

3. Place the salmon skin-side down on a sheet pan lined with parchment paper. Drizzle half of the maple syrup mixture over the salmon, ensuring that the fillets are evenly coated.

4. Bake for 8 minutes. Place the bell peppers and mushrooms around the fish, and drizzle with the remaining maple syrup mixture. Bake for another 8 to 10 minutes, or until the salmon is tender and has reached your desired doneness.

5. Lift the fillets with a spatula, making sure not to remove the skin, and transfer to a serving dish with vegetables.

MUSSELS *and* CHORIZO *in* RED WINE SAUCE

SERVES 2 • PREP TIME 10 minutes • COOK TIME 20 minutes

This recipe is perfect for celebrating a special night during the week. The simple ingredients come together perfectly to create a delicious meal that you likely had thought impossible to make yourself. Keep things simple: pair this dish with a glass of red wine and serve with a simple salad.

½ POUND CHORIZO, CASINGS REMOVED, CRUMBLED

1 LARGE ONION, SLICED

SEA SALT

FRESHLY GROUND BLACK PEPPER

1 POUND BLACK MUSSELS, CLEANED AND BEARDED

1 BOTTLE DRY RED WINE

Optional Add-ins

¼ CUP FRESH PARSLEY, CHOPPED, FOR GARNISH

1. In a large pot over high heat, cook the chorizo for 5 to 8 minutes, or until browned. Using a slotted spoon, remove the chorizo and set aside.

2. Add the onion and sauté for 3 to 4 minutes. Return the chorizo to the pot, and season with salt and pepper.

3. Add the mussels and wine. Cover the pot and bring to a boil. Cook until the mussels open, about 5 minutes.

4. Discard any mussels that have not opened. Stir well until the mussels are evenly coated with the wine and chorizo mixture.

6

5.

MEAT

Thirty-Minute Meatballs   88

Simple Beef Chili   89

Pork Fried Rice   90

Beef and Broccoli   91

Mushroom Bolognese   92

Sheet-Pan Steak and Veggies   93

Maple Pork and Pears   94

Steak Frites   95

Beef Tenderloin with Cauliflower and Kale   96

Sausage and Roasted Veggies   97

Stuffed Zucchini Boats   98

Southwest Stuffed Peppers   99

Tangy Orange Lamb Chops   100

Open-Faced Bacon and Brussels Burger   101

Beef and Tomato Skewers   102

THIRTY-MINUTE MEATBALLS (OPPOSITE), PAGE 88

THIRTY-MINUTE MEATBALLS

SERVES 2 • PREP TIME 10 minutes • COOK TIME 20 minutes

Making meatballs used to be an all-day affair. Unfortunately, there's just no time for that during the week, so we created this 30-minute recipe for those nights when you're craving meatballs but need to get dinner on the table in minutes. I like to serve these meatballs grain-free with only marinara sauce, you can also serve them on a bed of spaghetti. Just don't forget the Parmesan cheese and basil garnish!

½ POUND GROUND BEEF

½ YELLOW ONION, FINELY CHOPPED

¼ CUP ALMOND FLOUR

1 TEASPOON GARLIC POWDER

2 TEASPOONS ITALIAN SEASONING

SEA SALT

FRESHLY GROUND BLACK PEPPER

Optional Add-ins

MARINARA SAUCE, FOR SERVING

CHOPPED BASIL, FOR SERVING

PARMESAN CHEESE, FOR SERVING

1. Preheat the oven to 400°F.

2. In a large bowl, combine the ground beef, onion, almond flour, garlic powder and Italian seasoning, and season with salt and pepper.

3. Line a sheet pan with parchment paper. Form the beef mixture into 6 to 8 meatballs, and place them on the pan.

4. Bake until browned, about 20 minutes.

SIMPLE BEEF CHILI

SERVES 2 • PREP TIME 5 minutes • COOK TIME 25 minutes

All good home cooks have a meal they can pull together with their eyes closed—a recipe they know by heart, as if based on muscle memory. This chili is my go-to recipe, and it may soon become yours. We always keep these five ingredients on hand. Perfect for nights when we lack inspiration or spare time, this recipe never disappoints. Top it off with a drizzle of plain Greek yogurt and chopped green onions for a little added flair.

½ POUND GROUND BEEF

½ WHITE ONION, DICED

1 (15-OUNCE) CANS DICED TOMATOES WITH
    GREEN CHILES

1 (15-OUNCE) CANS BLACK BEANS, DRAINED
    AND RINSED

1 TABLESPOON CHILI POWDER

SEA SALT

FRESHLY GROUND BLACK PEPPER

Optional Add-ins

CHOPPED GREEN ONIONS, FOR GARNISH

GREEK YOGURT

1. In a large pot over medium-high heat, cook the ground beef for 8 to 10 minutes, stirring frequently, until it has browned. Using a slotted spoon, remove the ground beef from the pot and set aside.

2. Add the onion to the pot and sauté for 3 to 4 minutes, until soft. Return the beef to the pot and add the tomatoes, beans, and chili powder. Season with salt and pepper and stir well to combine.

3. Bring the chili to a boil. Reduce the heat to medium-low, cover, and simmer for 10 minutes.

INGREDIENT SWAP: You can easily swap the beef in this recipe for ground turkey. Be sure to add 1 tablespoon of olive oil before cooking the turkey to help it brown, and then another tablespoon of olive oil to cook the onion.

PORK FRIED RICE

SERVES 2 • PREP TIME 5 minutes • COOK TIME 25 minutes

Chances are that when you get a craving for Chinese food, fried rice is one of the dishes you are sure to order. Did you know that this take-out favorite takes less time to make at home than it does to get delivered? And it doesn't hurt that the homemade contains fresher ingredients. Want to pack in even more vegetables? Swap the brown rice for riced cauliflower!

2 TABLESPOONS EXTRA-VIRGIN OLIVE OIL,
    DIVIDED
½ POUND BONELESS PORK CHOPS, CUT
    INTO STRIPS
FRESHLY GROUND BLACK PEPPER
1 CUP FROZEN MIXED VEGETABLES
2 LARGE EGGS, LIGHTLY BEATEN
2 CUPS COOKED BROWN RICE
¼ CUP TAMARI

Optional Add-ins
CHOPPED GREEN ONIONS, FOR GARNISH

1. In a large nonstick pan, heat 1 tablespoon of olive oil over medium-high heat. Season the pork with pepper, and place on the pan. Cook each side for 4 to 5 minutes, or until cooked to desired doneness. Remove from the pan and set aside.

2. In the same pan, heat ½ tablespoon of olive oil. Add the mixed vegetables and sauté for 3 to 4 minutes, or until tender. Remove the veggies from the pan and set aside.

3. Heat the remaining olive oil in the pan. Add the eggs and cook until they begin to set, about 1 minute. Cook, for another minute, stirring occasionally.

4. Add the pork, veggies, and rice and cook for 2 minutes, stirring frequently. Add the tamari, stir thoroughly to combine, and cook for another 2 minutes.

DID YOU KNOW? If you don't have tamari on hand, it can be easily substituted with regular soy sauce or coconut aminos.

BEEF *and* BROCCOLI

SERVES 2 • PREP TIME 15 minutes • COOK TIME 10 minutes

This is another "takeout fake-out" recipe that Julien and I like to cook when we're craving Chinese food. Like the Pork Fried Rice (see page 90), this homemade dish is cheaper and takes less time to prepare than restaurant delivery, and since you're cooking at home, you can use quality ingredients. Sticky-sweet and perfectly salty, you won't be able to tell the difference between this version and your favorite restaurant's. Give your dinner a fun flair by serving it in takeout boxes and using chopsticks!

½ POUND FLANK STEAK, CUT INTO ¼-INCH-
   THICK PIECES
1 TABLESPOON TAPIOCA FLOUR
SEA SALT
FRESHLY GROUND BLACK PEPPER
2 TABLESPOONS OLIVE OIL, DIVIDED
1 HEAD BROCCOLI, CUT INTO FLORETS
¾ CUP WATER, DIVIDED
½ TABLESPOON MINCED FRESH GINGER
1½ TABLESPOONS TAMARI

Optional Add-ins
CHOPPED GREEN ONIONS, FOR GARNISH
TOASTED SESAME SEEDS, FOR GARNISH

1. In a large bowl, coat the beef in the tapioca flour. Season with salt and pepper and toss to coat evenly.

2. In a large cast-iron skillet, heat 1 tablespoon of olive oil over high heat, add the broccoli florets, and cook for 2 minutes, stirring frequently. Add ¼ cup of water and stir until the water evaporates. Remove the broccoli from the skillet and set aside.

3. Heat the remaining olive oil in the skillet, add ginger, and sauté for 1 to 2 minutes. Add the beef mixture and cook for 3 minutes, stirring continuously.

4. Add the tamari and remaining water, and bring to a simmer, stirring continuously until the sauce has thickened. Add the broccoli and cook for 2 more minutes.

PAIR UP: Serve this dish with lo mein egg noodles, whole-wheat spaghetti, or spiralized carrots and zucchini to turn this dish into beef and broccoli lo mein.

MUSHROOM BOLOGNESE

SERVES 2 • PREP TIME 5 minutes • COOK TIME 25 minutes

You know you've made good Bolognese when you devour it straight from the pot before you've even ladled it on top of your pasta. When I was young and my grandmother made Bolognese, I would always request a separate bowl to dunk my bread in until the bowl was wiped clean. This mushroom Bolognese can be eaten alone, but also makes a delicious topping to your favorite pasta or spiralized veggies.

1 TABLESPOON OLIVE OIL

2 GARLIC CLOVES, MINCED

4 OUNCES CHOPPED BABY BELLA MUSHROOMS

½ POUND GROUND BEEF

1 (15-OUNCE) CAN TOMATO SAUCE

1 TEASPOON DRIED OREGANO

Optional Add-in

1 BUTTERNUT SQUASH, SPIRALIZED INTO
    FETTUCCINI NOODLES

1. In a large pot, over medium-high heat sauté the garlic for 1 to 2 minutes. Add the mushrooms and stir to combine. Cook for 2 minutes.

2. Add the ground beef and cook for 8 to 10 minutes, break up with a spoon, and stir until it reaches desired doneness.

3. Add the tomato sauce and dried oregano. Season with salt and pepper, and stir to combine.

4. Reduce the heat to medium-low, cover, and simmer for 10 minutes.

SHEET-PAN STEAK *and* VEGGIES

SERVES 2 • PREP TIME 15 minutes • COOK TIME 15 minutes

I have at least six sheet pans in my cupboard. This may seem silly since I can use only two at a time in the oven, but they are so versatile that I always find myself reaching for one. Whether I am making homemade fruit leather, freezing chocolate bark, or baking cookies, the sheet pan rises to the challenge. And luckily, it's the only equipment you need to pull off a full steak and veggie dinner. To save on cleanup, be sure to line your sheet pan with aluminum foil first.

2 QUARTS WATER

1 POUND FINGERLING POTATOES, HALVED

8 OUNCES ASPARAGUS, ENDS TRIMMED

1 TABLESPOON EXTRA-VIRGIN OLIVE OIL

2 GARLIC CLOVES, MINCED

1 TEASPOON DRIED THYME

SEA SALT

FRESHLY GROUND BLACK PEPPER

½ POUND TOP SIRLOIN STEAK, 1-INCH THICK

1. Place the oven rack in the upper third of the oven, and preheat the broiler.

2. In a large pot over medium heat, bring the water to a boil. Add the potatoes and cook for 10 to 12 minutes, or until parboiled. Drain well.

3. Arrange the potatoes and asparagus on a sheet pan. Add the olive oil, minced garlic, and thyme. Season with salt and pepper, and toss to coat evenly.

4. Pat the steak dry, and season with salt and pepper. Arrange the steak in the center of the sheet pan with the veggies scattered around it.

5. Place into the oven, and broil each side of the steak for 4 to 5 minutes, or until it's browned and charred at the edges.

DID YOU KNOW? By tossing the vegetables with olive oil on the sheet pan, you are lightly greasing the sheet pan to prepare for the steak. If the sheet pan is not lightly greased, add a little more olive oil before adding the steak.

MAPLE PORK *and* PEARS

SERVES 2 • PREP TIME 5 minutes • COOK TIME 15 minutes

Like roasting a chicken, making pork chops is a skill that all chefs—even novices—should master. This recipe is perfect for beginners, but is a far cry from your mom's pork chops and applesauce. A twist on an old classic, this dish packs a savory-sweet punch thanks to the fresh pears and carrots, and a touch of maple syrup.

1 TABLESPOON BUTTER

2 PORK CHOPS, ½-INCH THICK

SEA SALT

FRESHLY GROUND BLACK PEPPER

6 MINI CARROTS WITH TOPS, HALVED
    LENGTHWISE

1 PEAR, CORED AND SLICED

3 TABLESPOONS PURE MAPLE SYRUP

1. In a large cast-iron skillet, melt the butter over medium heat. Generously season the pork with salt and pepper. Add the pork to the skillet and cook each side for 2 minutes, until golden brown.

2. Reduce the heat to medium-low. Add the carrots, pear, and maple syrup. Cover and simmer for 8 minutes, or until the pork chops are fully cooked.

3. Remove the chops, carrots, and pear from the skillet. Bring the maple syrup to a boil. Cook uncovered for 1 to 2 minutes, or until thickened. Drizzle the syrup over the pork chops and serve.

STEAK FRITES

SERVES 2 • PREP TIME 5 minutes • COOK TIME 25 minutes

The best weeknight dinners require as little work as possible without sacrificing flavor. This is my version of steak frites, a simple broiled steak paired with perfectly seasoned potatoes—all cooked on a single pan. It might seem impossible, but the truth is that steak frites cooked at home have never been easier or more delicious. The key to this dish is to fully cook the potatoes before adding them to the steak and sticking the combo under the broiler.

2 RUSSET POTATOES CUT INTO THICK STRIPS
2 TABLESPOONS OLIVE OIL, DIVIDED
2 GARLIC CLOVES, MINCED
1 TEASPOON DRIED THYME
¼ CUP PARMESAN CHEESE
SEA SALT
FRESHLY GROUND BLACK PEPPER
2 (1-INCH-THICK) TOP SIRLOIN STEAK

1. Preheat the oven to 450°F.

2. Arrange the potatoes on one side of a sheet pan. Add 1 tablespoon of olive oil and the garlic, thyme, and Parmesan cheese. Season with salt and pepper, and toss to coat evenly. Bake for 12 to 14 minutes, or until golden brown, tossing occasionally.

3. Remove the sheet pan from the oven, and preheat the oven to broil. Pat the steak dry and season it with salt and pepper. Lightly coat the sheet pan with the remaining olive oil. Add the steak.

4. Place the pan in the oven and broil each side for 4 to 5 minutes, or until the steak is browned and charred at the edges.

DID YOU KNOW? Cut your prep time by swapping the russet potatoes for baby potatoes. They can be added directly to the pan and get nice and crispy on the outside while staying tender inside.

BEEF TENDERLOIN with CAULIFLOWER and KALE

SERVES 2 • PREP TIME 10 minutes • COOK TIME 25 minutes

Beef tenderloin is the classic choice for an extravagant holiday dinner, but it is just as impressive and delicious when made for two. Although cooking the tenderloin is relatively simple, it is important to prep it properly. Have your butcher trim the tenderloin to remove the silver skin–that thick layer of white tissue running along the surface of the meat.

1 WHOLE BEEF FILET (ABOUT 1 POUND), TRIMMED

3 TABLESPOONS EXTRA-VIRGIN OLIVE OIL, DIVIDED

SEA SALT

FRESHLY GROUND BLACK PEPPER

½ HEAD CAULIFLOWER, CUT INTO FLORETS

2 LARGE SHALLOTS, SLICED

2 TABLESPOONS FRESHLY SQUEEZED LEMON JUICE

2 CUPS BABY KALE

1. Preheat the oven to 475°F.

2. To ensure even cooking, tie up the filet with butcher's twine (or a similar string) so that it's in a round shape. Place the beef on a sheet pan lined with aluminum foil. Rub the beef with 1 tablespoon of olive oil, and season with salt and pepper. Bake for 10 minutes.

3. In a large bowl, toss to combine cauliflower, shallots, and 1 tablespoon of olive oil. Season with salt and pepper. Remove the sheet pan from the oven, and arrange the vegetables around the beef. Bake for about 10 to 15 minutes, or until the meat reaches desired doneness.

4. Remove the beef from the sheet pan, and cover it with aluminum foil. Let it stand for about 10 minutes.

5. Whisk together the remaining olive oil and lemon juice. Season with salt and pepper. Stir the kale into the vegetables on the hot sheet pan. Drizzle with the olive oil mixture.

6. Remove the string and slice the filet. Serve with the veggies on the side.

DID YOU KNOW? To get the most flavor out of the beef, be sure to generously coat the filet with sea salt. You can also use dried herbs and/or crushed garlic for added flavor.

SAUSAGE *and* ROASTED VEGGIES

SERVES 2 • PREP TIME 5 minutes • COOK TIME 30 minutes

This vegetable and sausage combination is something of an "everything but the kitchen sink" recipe inspired by an empty fridge late at night. You know, when you come home from a long day at work ready for dinner, only to find random leftover ingredients in the fridge? Simply chop a few veggies, toss them with olive oil, add whatever sausage you have on hand, and voilà—dinner!

½ POUND BUTTERNUT SQUASH, CUBED

½ POUND BRUSSELS SPROUTS, ENDS TRIMMED
   AND HALVED

1 YELLOW ONION, SLICED THICK

1 TABLESPOON OLIVE OIL

½ TEASPOON CRUSHED RED PEPPER FLAKES

SEA SALT

FRESHLY GROUND BLACK PEPPER

½ POUND SWEET ITALIAN SAUSAGE

1. Preheat oven to 400°F.

2. Arrange the butternut squash, Brussels sprouts, and onion on a sheet pan. Drizzle with the olive oil and toss to coat evenly. Sprinkle with the red pepper flakes, and season with salt and pepper. Place the sausage between the veggies.

3. Bake for 15 minutes, flip the sausage, and cook for another 10 to 15 minutes, or until the veggies are tender and the sausage begins to brown.

STUFFED ZUCCHINI BOATS

SERVES 2 • PREP TIME 5 minutes • COOK TIME 30 minutes

Chances are your social media feeds are loaded with photos of zucchini boats. I was late to catch on to the zucchini boat fad, but who cares if you're late to the party when the treats taste this good? To keep it classic, these zucchini boats rely on simple Italian-inspired flavors. For a personal touch, you can experiment with flavors by using different proteins.

2 ZUCCHINIS, ENDS TRIMMED

1 TABLESPOON EXTRA-VIRGIN OLIVE OIL

½ ONION, CHOPPED

½ POUND GROUND BEEF

1 CUP MARINARA SAUCE

SEA SALT

FRESHLY GROUND BLACK PEPPER

¼ CUP SHREDDED MOZZARELLA CHEESE

1. Preheat oven to 450°F.

2. Cut each zucchini in half lengthwise and scoop out the inside, leaving a ½-inch-thick shell. Roughly chop up the zucchini pulp.

3. To make the Bolognese sauce, heat the olive oil in a nonstick pan over medium heat. Add the onion and sauté for 1 to 2 minutes. Add the zucchini pulp and ground beef. Cook for 5 to 8 minutes, or until browned.

4. Add the marinara sauce to the pan, stir well, and bring to a simmer. Season with salt and pepper.

5. Season the zucchini shells with salt and pepper, then fill each one with the Bolognese mixture. Bake for 15 minutes, top with the mozzarella cheese, and bake for another 5 minutes, or until the cheese is melted.

SOUTHWEST STUFFED PEPPERS

SERVES 2 • PREP TIME 5 minutes • COOK TIME 25 minutes

Stuffed peppers are one of those classic comfort foods most likely born from a need to use up leftovers. Most versions call for ground beef and leftover grains, but like so many classic recipes, everyone seems to have their own spin. I added a little Southwest flair to this rendition with fresh salsa and pepper Jack cheese. You can also stir in some chili powder and black beans if you have them on hand.

½ CUP QUINOA

2 QUARTS WATER, PLUS 1 CUP

½ POUND GROUND BEEF

SEA SALT

FRESHLY GROUND BLACK PEPPER

2 BELL PEPPERS, TOPS CUT OFF AND CORES
    REMOVED

¼ CUP SALSA

¼ CUP PEPPER JACK CHEESE

Optional Add-Ins

AVOCADO, DICED

FRESH CILANTRO, CHOPPED

RED ONION, DICED

1. In a large pot, add the quinoa and 1 cup of water, and bring to a boil over high heat, stirring frequently. Reduce the heat to low and cook let simmer for 15 to 20 minutes, stirring occasionally.

2. Meanwhile, in a nonstick pan over medium heat, cook the ground beef for 5 to 8 minutes, or until browned.

3. In another large pot, bring the remaining 2 quarts of water to a boil. Add the bell peppers and blanch for 3 to 5 minutes. Carefully remove the peppers one by one using tongs, and place them in an oven-safe dish.

4. Once the liquid is absorbed and the quinoa is tender, remove it from the heat. Use a fork to fluff the quinoa, transfer it into a large bowl and let cool.

5. Using a slotted spoon, add the ground beef to the bowl of quinoa. Add the salsa and stir until evenly mixed. Carefully spoon the mixture into the bell peppers. Top with the pepper Jack cheese.

6. Preheat the oven to broil. Once heated, place the peppers in the oven and cook for 3 to 4 minutes, or until the cheese is melted and golden brown.

TANGY ORANGE LAMB CHOPS

SERVES 2 • PREP TIME 15 minutes • COOK TIME 10 minutes

I love creating unique flavors from simple, fresh ingredients. In this recipe, the juice and zest from an orange create a tangy marinade that pairs perfectly with the lamb chops. And after I juice and zest the orange, I like to snack on the leftovers, or add the orange leftovers to the skillet when boiling the balsamic vinegar. Serve the lamb chops with a side of broccoli or a simple garden salad.

2 TEASPOONS OLIVE OIL, DIVIDED

1 TABLESPOON FRESHLY SQUEEZED ORANGE JUICE

1 TEASPOON ORANGE ZEST

4 (4-OUNCE) LAMB CHOPS, TRIMMED

SEA SALT

FRESHLY GROUND BLACK PEPPER

1½ TABLESPOONS BALSAMIC VINEGAR

1. In a large plastic bag, combine 1 teaspoon of olive oil, the orange juice, and the orange zest. Place the lamb chops in the bag and toss to coat evenly. Let stand for 10 minutes.

2. Remove the lamb from the bag, and season generously with salt and pepper.

3. In a cast-iron skillet, heat the remaining olive oil over medium-high heat. Add the lamb to the skillet, and cook each side for 2 minutes, or until it reaches desired doneness. Remove from the skillet.

4. In a nonstick pan, heat the balsamic vinegar over medium-high heat. Bring to a boil and cook for 2 to 3 minutes, or until the vinegar is syrupy. Drizzle over the lamb just before serving.

OPEN-FACED BACON *and* BRUSSELS BURGER

SERVES 2 • PREP TIME 5 minutes • COOK TIME 20 minutes

We default to burgers for dinner at least once a week. They are an easy option because we always have ground beef in the fridge, plus they are easy to customize by using a variety of toppings. The spices added to the meat, along with the crispy Brussels sprout topping, make this burger feel like a gourmet meal rather than just another burger.

½ POUND BRUSSELS SPROUTS, ENDS TRIMMED
    AND THINLY SLICED
1 TABLESPOON OLIVE OIL
SEA SALT
FRESHLY GROUND BLACK PEPPER
½ POUND GROUND BEEF
¼ TEASPOON DRIED ROSEMARY
¼ TEASPOON DRIED THYME

Optional Add-ins
COOKED BACON
CARAMELIZED ONION

1. In a large bowl, add the Brussels sprouts and olive oil. Season with salt and pepper, and toss until well combined. Spread the seasoned Brussels sprouts onto a sheet pan lined with aluminum foil. Bake for 20 minutes, tossing half way through.

2. Meanwhile, heat the grill or a grill pan on the stove over medium heat.

3. In a large bowl, combine the ground beef, rosemary, and thyme. Season with salt and pepper, and mix until well combined. Form the ground beef into two patties.

4. Grill the patties, about 4 minutes on each side. The burger patties should be deep brown and fully cooked on the outside, and slightly pink on the inside.

5. Top each burger with a generous pile of the crispy shaved Brussels sprouts.

BEEF *and* TOMATO SKEWERS

SERVES 2 • PREP TIME 10 minutes • COOK TIME 10 minutes

Skewers are a super simple way to spice up your average weeknight meal. Julien and I like to see who can thread their skewers the fastest. The winner gets to enjoy a glass of wine, while the loser is forced to tend the grill. In the end we are both winners, because in less than 10 minutes we're enjoying the juicy tomatoes and flavorful steak together. Serve these skewers on top of rice or with a simple salad.

2 TABLESPOONS BALSAMIC VINAIGRETTE
2 TABLESPOONS BARBECUE SAUCE
½ TEASPOON DIJON MUSTARD
½ POUND TOP SIRLOIN STEAK, CUT INTO
    1-INCH CUBES
1 CUP CHERRY TOMATOES

1. Heat the grill to medium heat.

2. In a large bowl, whisk together the balsamic vinaigrette, barbecue sauce, and Dijon mustard, until well combined. In a separate bowl, set aside 2 tablespoons of this mixture. Add the steak to remaining mixture, tossing to evenly coat the meat.

3. Thread the steak cubes and cherry tomatoes together on the skewers.

4. Place the skewers on the grill and cook for 6 to 8 minutes, turning occasionally and basting with the reserved sauce, until the beef reaches desired doneness.

❧DON'T WASTE❧

To make the most of your budget, the following are my tips for preserving ingredients that often go to waste, so that you don't throw away money or food.

IN THE PANTRY

DRIED HERBS AND SPICES Whole spices last much longer than crushed or ground spices. They can be kept for up to two years, while ground spices should be replaced every six months. Store your dried herbs and spices in airtight containers in a dark, cool pantry.

NUTS AND SEEDS Store nuts and seeds in a dark, cool pantry to preserve their nutrients and keep them fresh.

IN THE FRIDGE

CHEESE Cheese should be wrapped and stored in porous material such as waxed or parchment paper. Avoid plastic wrap. Each cheese should be wrapped separately and marked with the name and date of purchase.

EGGS Store-bought eggs should be stored in their cartons on a shelf.

FRESH HERBS Fresh water-based herbs like basil, parsley, and cilantro should be treated like flowers. When you bring them home, remove any twist ties, trim a small amount off the stem ends, and store them in a glass of water. Cover the herbs loosely with a plastic bag, and they'll stay fresh for at least a week.

MUSHROOMS Prepackaged mushrooms are best left in their original packaging. Once you do open them, wrap the whole package in plastic wrap if you don't use them all. However, wild mushrooms are best kept in a paper bag in your refrigerator's crisper.

ON THE COUNTER

GARLIC, ONIONS, AND SHALLOTS These vegetables will turn mealy and lose their flavor in the fridge. Store them on the counter and out of the sun.

TOMATOES, POTATOES, AND WINTER SQUASH These vegetables should also be stored in a cool, dry place instead of the fridge. Be sure to keep your potatoes away from onions, as gases from the onions can hasten sprouting in potatoes.

7

5.

POULTRY

Simple Chicken Piccata   106

Chicken and Broccoli   107

Chicken Tikka Masala   108

Cilantro-Lime Chicken   109

Asian Chicken Lettuce Wraps   110

Rice Bowl with Thai-Basil
Chicken   111

Lemon-Rosemary Chicken
with Broccolini   112

Shredded Chicken Tacos   113

Potato Stuffed with Broccoli,
Cheddar, and Chicken   114

Chicken Thighs with Tomatoes
and Asparagus   116

Easy Chicken Marsala   117

Herbed Chicken and Potatoes   118

Turkey Steaks with Mushrooms   119

Spinach-Turkey Burger   120

Chicken and Veggie Skewers   121

CHICKEN THIGHS WITH TOMATOES AND ASPARAGUS (OPPOSITE), PAGE 116

SIMPLE CHICKEN PICCATA

SERVES 2 • PREP TIME 5 minutes • COOK TIME 20 minutes

This piccata was one of the first recipes I mastered when Julien and I started living together—so much so that I probably made it way too often in those first few months. Now we make it less frequently, but when we do, it's a reminder of that special time in our lives. I like to complete this dish with a side of roasted veggies or a simple salad.

1 TABLESPOON EXTRA-VIRGIN OLIVE OIL

2 BONELESS CHICKEN BREASTS (ABOUT ¼ POUND EACH)

SEA SALT

FRESHLY GROUND BLACK PEPPER

1 GARLIC CLOVE, MINCED

¼ CUP CHICKEN BROTH

1 LEMON, SLICED

1 TABLESPOON CAPERS

1. In a large cast-iron skillet, heat the olive oil over medium-high heat. Season the chicken with salt and pepper.

2. Place the chicken in the skillet and cook each side for 6 to 8 minutes, or until browned. Remove the chicken from the skillet.

3. Add the garlic to the skillet and sauté it for 30 seconds, or until lightly browned. Add the chicken broth and bring it to a boil, scraping the skillet to loosen the browned bits from the bottom.

4. Add the lemon slices and capers. Cover the skillet and reduce the heat to low. Cook for 4 to 5 minutes, or until the lemon slices are softened.

5. Return the chicken to the skillet to heat, and serve with the sauce, lemon slices, and capers on top.

DID YOU KNOW? If you have a little extra time, try breading the chicken before putting it on the skillet. Dredge the chicken breasts in an egg wash, and then coat them evenly with almond meal.

CHICKEN *and* BROCCOLI

SERVES 2 • PREP TIME 5 minutes • COOK TIME 15 minutes

Like many of the other takeout-inspired dishes in this book, this chicken classic comes together in under 20 minutes. That means you can have dinner on the table in less time than it would take to get it delivered from a restaurant! The simple ingredients are full of flavor and often healthier than those in takeout dishes, so this meal comes with less guilt, too. To make it extra filling, don't forget the rice on the side!

½ TABLESPOON EXTRA-VIRGIN OLIVE OIL

2 GARLIC CLOVES, MINCED

½ TABLESPOON FRESH MINCED GINGER

2 BONELESS CHICKEN BREASTS (ABOUT ¼ POUND EACH), DICED

2 TABLESPOONS TAMARI

1 SMALL HEAD BROCCOLI, TRIMMED INTO FLORETS

Optional Add-in
BROWN RICE, FOR SERVING

1. In a large cast-iron skillet, heat the olive oil over medium-high heat. Add the garlic and ginger to the skillet, and cook for about 1 minute, or until lightly browned.

2. Add the chicken and tamari, and cook for 8 to 10 minutes, stirring occasionally, until browned.

3. Add the broccoli florets and cook for 4 to 5 minutes, or until tender.

INGREDIENT SWAP: I love the combination of crisp broccoli and tender chicken in this recipe, but you can easily swap the broccoli for carrots or green beans. A bag of frozen mixed vegetables also works great—just add a bit more garlic, ginger, and tamari to ensure that the chicken and vegetables are evenly seasoned.

CHICKEN TIKKA MASALA

SERVES 2 • PREP TIME 10 minutes • COOK TIME 20 minutes

When I told Julien I was working on a tikka masala recipe for this book, he was very surprised. Julien loves the bold flavors and strong spices of Indian cuisine, but I've never been too big a fan. So he usually ends up cooking Indian dishes when I am traveling or out for the night with girlfriends. This recipe is packed with flavor and perfect for Indian food enthusiasts like Julien, but mild enough for those less enthusiastic like me. It is sure to become a favorite in your house like it has in ours.

2 BONELESS CHICKEN BREASTS (ABOUT
    ¼ POUND EACH), DICED
2 TABLESPOONS MASALA PASTE, DIVIDED
¼ CUP PLAIN GREEK YOGURT
½ CUP CANNED TOMATO PURÉE
1 CUP FULL-FAT COCONUT MILK
SEA SALT

Optional Add-ins
BASMATI RICE, FOR SERVING
CILANTRO, FOR GARNISH

1. In a large plastic bag, combine the chicken, ½ tablespoon of masala paste, and the Greek yogurt. Shake until the chicken is evenly coated and let it marinate in the fridge for 10 to 15 minutes.

2. Heat a large cast-iron skillet over medium-high heat. Add the remaining masala paste and cook for 2 to 3 minutes, stirring frequently.

3. Add the chicken and cook for 5 to 8 minutes, stirring occasionally, until fully cooked.

4. Add the tomato purée and coconut milk, and simmer for 15 minutes. Season with salt and let stand for about 4 to 5 minutes, or until the sauce begins to thicken.

DID YOU KNOW? Masala paste is widely available but can be substituted with curry paste if you are unable to find it at your local market. Alternatively, if you prefer to make a homemade version, you can visit my website (KenzieSwanhart.com) for a recipe made from vegetables, herbs, and spices.

CILANTRO-LIME CHICKEN

SERVES 2 • PREP TIME 5 minutes • COOK TIME 10 minutes

*There is nothing exciting about coming home
to make a boring chicken dish at the end of
a long day. But add a creamy and flavorful
cilantro-lime sauce, and your boring weeknight
meal will be transformed. I personally like to
serve this chicken over a bed of rice to soak up
the sauce, but quinoa and farro work great, too.*

1 TABLESPOON EXTRA-VIRGIN OLIVE OIL

2 BONELESS CHICKEN BREASTS (ABOUT
    ¼ POUND EACH)

½ AVOCADO

JUICE OF ½ LIME

¼ CUP FULL-FAT COCONUT MILK

⅓ CUP CILANTRO

SEA SALT

Optional Add-in

BROWN RICE, FOR SERVING

1. In a large cast-iron skillet, heat the olive oil over medium-high heat. Add the chicken and cook each side for 6 to 8 minutes, or until browned and fully cooked.

2. Meanwhile, in a food processor, combine the avocado, lime juice, coconut milk, and cilantro. Pulse the mixture until smooth. Season with salt.

3. When the chicken is cooked, remove it from the skillet and drizzle with the cilantro-lime sauce.

ASIAN CHICKEN LETTUCE WRAPS

SERVES 2 • PREP TIME 10 minutes • COOK TIME 15 minutes

Julien and I love trying new recipes, but we usually reserve them for the weekend because they often take longer than expected. We've tried many recipes for chicken lettuce wraps. While many of them are delicious, they all take a ton of time to prepare. So I decided to make my own! This version requires minimal prep and chopping, but doesn't skimp on flavor. If you don't like mushrooms, change them for diced red bell pepper.

2 TABLESPOONS EXTRA-VIRGIN OLIVE OIL, DIVIDED

2 GARLIC CLOVES, MINCED

½ POUND GROUND CHICKEN

3 TABLESPOONS TAMARI

4 OUNCES BABY BELLA MUSHROOMS,
    FINELY CHOPPED

SEA SALT

FRESHLY GROUND BLACK PEPPER

4 LARGE ROMAINE LETTUCE LEAVES

Optional Add-Ins

SCALLIONS, THINLY SLICED

CRUSHED PEANUTS

SESAME SEEDS

1. In a large cast-iron skillet, heat 1 tablespoon of olive oil over medium-high heat. Add garlic and cook for about 30 seconds, or until lightly browned.

2. Add the ground chicken to the skillet and cook for 6 to 8 minutes, stirring occasionally, until browned. Add the tamari and stir well. Cook for another 2 minutes, then remove the chicken from the skillet and set aside.

3. Add remaining olive oil and mushrooms to the skillet. Cook for 3 to 4 minutes, stirring occasionally.

4. When the mushrooms are fully cooked, return the chicken mixture to the skillet. Season with salt and pepper, and cook for another 2 to 3 minutes.

5. Divide the chicken evenly among the lettuce leaves and fold each one up into a wrap.

DID YOU KNOW? For added flavor add 1 diced shallot and ½ tablespoon of minced ginger to the skillet with the garlic.

RICE BOWL *with* THAI-BASIL CHICKEN

SERVES 2 • PREP TIME 10 minutes • COOK TIME 15 minutes

If you've read my cookbook Clean Eating Bowls, *then you know I love a good grain bowl. Inspired by Thai cuisine, this recipe brings ginger and basil together perfectly to complement the hearty rice and tender chicken. Add carrots, bell peppers, and green onions to pack in even more nutrients.*

1 CUP BROWN RICE

1 TABLESPOON EXTRA-VIRGIN OLIVE OIL, DIVIDED

½ POUND GROUND CHICKEN

1 TEASPOON GROUND GINGER

3 TABLESPOONS TAMARI

1 CUP THAI BASIL LEAVES

SEA SALT

FRESHLY GROUND BLACK PEPPER

Optional Add-ins

LIME JUICE AND WEDGES, FOR GARNISH

THINLY SLICED SCALLIONS, FOR GARNISH

SESAME SEEDS, FOR GARNISH

1. Prepare the rice according to the package. Set aside.

2. In a large cast-iron skillet, heat the olive oil over medium-high heat. Add the ground chicken to the skillet and cook for 6 to 8 minutes, stirring occasionally, until browned.

3. Season with the ginger and stir to combine. Add the tamari and stir well. Cook for another 2 to 3 minutes.

4. Add the Thai basil leaves and cook for 2 to 3 minutes, stirring occasionally, until the basil begins to wilt. Season with salt and pepper.

5. Divide the brown rice between two bowls and top with the basil chicken.

PAIR UP: For added heat, add a finely chopped red Thai chile to the chicken when you stir in the ground ginger. Be sure to remove the seeds so that the spice is not overpowering!

LEMON-ROSEMARY CHICKEN *with* BROCCOLINI

SERVES 2 • PREP TIME 10 minutes • COOK TIME 20 minutes

This is my go-to recipe when I don't know what to make for dinner. The simple ingredients come together to create a delicious and easy meal. Dinner will be on the table before you know it—you won't even remember doing any work!

1 TABLESPOON CHOPPED FRESH ROSEMARY

1 GARLIC CLOVE, MINCED

2 TABLESPOONS EXTRA-VIRGIN OLIVE OIL, DIVIDED

SEA SALT

FRESHLY GROUND BLACK PEPPER

1 LEMON, ½ SLICED AND ½ JUICED

2 CHICKEN BREASTS (ABOUT ½ POUND EACH), BONES AND SKIN INTACT

4 OUNCES BROCCOLINI

1. Preheat the oven to 425°F.

2. Combine the rosemary, garlic, and 1 tablespoon of olive oil in a bowl. Season with salt and black pepper.

3. Arrange the chicken on a sheet pan. Rub one quarter of the rosemary mixture beneath the skin of each chicken breast. Thinly slice one of the lemon halves, and place 2 lemon slices beneath the skin. Rub the outside of the chicken with the remaining rosemary mixture and set aside.

4. Put the broccolini in a plastic bag. Squeeze the juice of the remaining lemon half into the plastic bag and add the remaining olive oil. Sprinkle in salt and pepper, and shake the bag to coat evenly. Remove the seasoned broccolini from the bag, and place it on the sheet pan.

5. Place the sheet pan in the oven and roast for about 20 minutes, or until the chicken is cooked and the broccolini is lightly browned.

DID YOU KNOW? Chicken can cook differently depending on thickness. To ensure the chicken is fully cooked, insert a thermometer into the thickest portion of the chicken. It should read 165°F.

SHREDDED CHICKEN TACOS

SERVES 2 • PREP TIME 10 minutes • COOK TIME 20 minutes

These tacos are the perfect dinner for our Taco Tuesdays. Cook the chicken and set up a little taco bar so that you and your significant other can assemble the perfect taco with all the fixings. This recipe serves two, but you can easily double the chicken and save half for another night. You can also use the extra shredded chicken for my Potato Stuffed with Broccoli, Cheddar, and Chicken recipe (see page 114).

2 BONELESS CHICKEN BREASTS (ABOUT
    ¼ POUND EACH)
2 CUPS WATER
1 TABLESPOON EXTRA-VIRGIN OLIVE OIL
½ TEASPOON GROUND CUMIN
½ TEASPOON CHILI POWDER
½ CUP DICED TOMATOES WITH CHILES
SEA SALT
FRESHLY GROUND BLACK PEPPER
4 SMALL CORN TORTILLAS

Optional Add-Ins
RED CABBAGE, SHREDDED
AVOCADO, DICED
QUESO FRESCO, CRUMBLED
FRESH CILANTRO

1. Place the chicken breasts in a large pot, and add enough water to cover the chicken. Bring to a boil over medium-high heat, and let simmer for about 10 to 15 minutes, until the chicken is cooked and no longer pink.

2. Transfer the chicken breasts to a large bowl, allow to cool, and shred using two forks.

3. In a nonstick pan, heat the olive oil over medium heat. Add the shredded chicken, cumin, chili powder, and diced tomatoes. Season with salt and pepper, and cook for 3 to 4 minutes.

4. Assemble the tacos by spooning the chicken on half a tortilla, and fold the other half on top of the filling. Top with other toppings as desired.

POTATO STUFFED *with* BROCCOLI, CHEDDAR, *and* CHICKEN

SERVES 2 • PREP TIME 10 minutes • COOK TIME 20 minutes

This recipe brings all my favorite foods into one dish. Broccoli? Yum! Cheddar cheese? Yum! Chicken? Yum! Potatoes? Double yum! What's not to love? Every single bite is filled with goodness.

1 BONELESS CHICKEN BREAST (ABOUT ½ POUND)

2 CUPS WATER

2 RUSSET POTATOES

¼ CUP PLAIN GREEK YOGURT

SEA SALT

FRESHLY GROUND BLACK PEPPER

½ CUP BROCCOLI FLORETS, CHOPPED

½ CUP CHEDDAR CHEESE, SHREDDED

1. Preheat oven to 450°F.

2. Place the chicken breasts in a large pot, and add enough water to cover the chicken. Bring to a boil over medium-high heat, and let simmer for about 10 minutes, or until the chicken is fully cooked and no longer pink.

3. Meanwhile, pierce the potatoes several times with a fork. Place them on a paper towel in the microwave, and cook each side for about 5 minutes, until they are tender. Remove the potatoes from the microwave, and let them cool for several minutes.

4. When the chicken is cooked, transfer it to a large bowl, allow to cool, and shred using two forks. Set aside.

5. Cut each potato in half lengthwise and scoop out the flesh. Place the flesh in a large bowl and mash it with a fork. Set the skins aside.

6. Add the Greek yogurt to the mashed potatoes, season with salt and pepper, and stir gently to combine. Add the shredded chicken, broccoli, and Cheddar cheese and stir until well combined.

7. Fill the potato skins with the mixture and place in the oven for 10 minutes, or until the cheese is melted and the filling is heated through.

COOKING TIP: Stuffed potatoes are a quick and delicious meal any day of the week. Prep in advance and bake a bunch of potatoes on a Sunday, which you can fill throughout the week with your favorite flavors. Toss in beans, veggies, and protein for a balanced meal in minutes.

CHICKEN THIGHS *with* TOMATOES *and* ASPARAGUS

SERVES 2 • PREP TIME 5 minutes • COOK TIME 25 minutes

Chicken thighs are incredibly juicy and flavorful. Best of all, they are often among the most inexpensive cuts of meat. In this recipe, the thighs are cooked in a cast-iron skillet—so that the skin gets nice and crispy—then paired with fresh veggies to pull the dish together. The flavors work wonderfully on their own, but this dish is also great served over quinoa.

3 TO 4 CHICKEN THIGHS, BONE AND SKIN INTACT

2 TABLESPOONS EXTRA-VIRGIN OLIVE OIL, DIVIDED

SEA SALT

FRESHLY GROUND BLACK PEPPER

8 OUNCES ASPARAGUS, ENDS TRIMMED

1 CUP GRAPE TOMATOES

JUICE OF 1 LEMON

½ LEMON CUT INTO QUARTERS

3 FRESH THYME SPRIGS

1. Preheat the oven to 400°F.

2. Coat chicken thighs with 1 tablespoon olive oil, and season generously with salt and pepper.

3. In a cast-iron skillet over medium heat, arrange the chicken in a single layer, skin-side down. Cook undisturbed for 10 to 15 minutes.

4. When the skin is crispy and brown, remove from the heat and place on a sheet pan skin-side up. Arrange the asparagus and tomatoes around the chicken thighs. Drizzle with remaining olive oil and lemon juice.

5. Scatter the thyme on top of the chicken, and place the baking sheet in the oven.

6. Roast for about 15 minutes, or until the chicken is fully cooked.

EASY CHICKEN MARSALA

SERVES 2 • PREP TIME 5 minutes • COOK TIME 15 minutes

When I go back to my hometown, we always order from a little Italian restaurant down the street. Their chicken marsala is my favorite, so this is the recipe I use to re-create it at home. Serve over angel hair pasta, cauliflower rice, or with a simple side salad.

1 TABLESPOON EXTRA-VIRGIN OLIVE OIL

2 BONELESS CHICKEN BREASTS (ABOUT
    ¼ POUND EACH)

SEA SALT

FRESHLY GROUND BLACK PEPPER

1 GARLIC CLOVE, MINCED

1 CUP SLICED CREMINI MUSHROOMS

¼ CUP MARSALA WINE

1 TABLESPOON BUTTER

1. In a large nonstick pan, heat the olive oil over medium-high heat. Season the chicken with salt and pepper.

2. Place the chicken in the pan and cook each side for 6 to 8 minutes, or until browned and fully cooked. Remove the chicken and set it aside.

3. Add the garlic and cook for 30 seconds, until lightly browned. Add the mushrooms and cook until tender, for about 2 minutes, stirring frequently.

4. Add the wine and cook for about 1 minute. Reduce the heat and add the butter. Stir until the butter melts.

5. Return the chicken to the pan and heat through. Serve the chicken topped with mushrooms and sauce.

INGREDIENT SWAP: Don't worry if you don't have marsala wine on hand. There are many ways to substitute it. For example, you can combine ¼ cup of grape juice and 1 teaspoon of brandy, or ¼ cup of dry white wine and 1 teaspoon of brandy. For a nonalcoholic version, combine ¼ cup of white grape juice, 1 tablespoon of vanilla extract, and 2 tablespoons of sherry vinegar. If you don't want to turn this recipe into a mixology class, simply substitute the marsala with pinot noir.

HERBED CHICKEN *and* POTATOES

SERVES 2 • PREP TIME 5 minutes • COOK TIME 25 minutes

Chicken and potatoes is a classic, hearty dinner dish. I like to use drumsticks and red bliss potatoes, but you can use whatever cut of meat you have in the freezer and whichever potatoes you have in the pantry. Likewise, while this recipe calls for classic Italian seasoning, you're welcome to try any seasoning blend you want. The base ingredients carry loads of flavor, no matter what seasoning you use.

4 CHICKEN DRUMSTICKS (ABOUT 1 POUND)
1 POUND RED BLISS POTATOES, HALVED
1 TABLESPOON EXTRA-VIRGIN OLIVE OIL
1 TABLESPOON ITALIAN SEASONING
SEA SALT
FRESHLY GROUND BLACK PEPPER

1. Preheat the oven to 400°F.

2. On a sheet pan lined with aluminum foil, arrange the drumsticks and potatoes in a single layer. Drizzle with the olive oil, and sprinkle with the Italian seasoning, salt, and pepper. Toss to coat evenly.

3. Bake for about 20 minutes, tossing occasionally, until the thickest part of the chicken is 165°F.

4. Place the sheet pan under the broiler for 2 to 3 minutes, until the chicken is golden brown and crispy.

INGREDIENT SWAP: I love using drumsticks in this recipe, but you can easily swap them for chicken breast, legs, or thighs if you prefer.

TURKEY STEAKS *with* MUSHROOMS

SERVES 2 • PREP TIME 5 minutes • COOK TIME 20 minutes

Turkey is often reserved for special occasions and holidays. But the truth is that it makes an easy meal any night of the week. You'll love the way this seasoned turkey pairs with the earthy flavors of sautéed mushrooms and spinach.

1 TURKEY BREAST TENDERLOIN
   (ABOUT ½ POUND)
SEA SALT
FRESHLY GROUND BLACK PEPPER
2 TABLESPOONS BUTTER, DIVIDED
2 GARLIC CLOVES, MINCED
1 CUP BUTTON MUSHROOMS, SLICED
3 CUPS BABY SPINACH

1. Slice the turkey tenderloin horizontally to make two ½-inch-thick steaks. Season generously with salt and pepper.

2. In large cast-iron skillet, melt 1 tablespoon of butter over medium-high heat. Add the turkey and cook for about 15 minutes, turning once, until it's no longer pink. Remove the turkey from the skillet.

3. Add the remaining butter and garlic to the skillet. Sauté for about 30 seconds. Add the mushrooms and cook for 3 to 4 minutes, stirring occasionally.

4. Add the spinach and cook for 1 to 2 minutes, stirring occasionally, until the spinach has wilted. Serve the turkey with mushrooms and spinach on the side.

SPINACH-TURKEY BURGER

SERVES 2 • PREP TIME 10 minutes • COOK TIME 15 minutes

Gourmet burgers are in style right now, but you don't need to be a fancy chef to get in on the action. These turkey burgers are packed with flavor but are super simple to make at home. All you need are a few simple ingredients. If you have a little extra time, cook bacon or caramelize onions to pile on top!

1 TEASPOON EXTRA-VIRGIN OLIVE OIL

2 GARLIC CLOVES, MINCED

2 CUPS BABY SPINACH

½ POUND LEAN GROUND TURKEY

2 OUNCES CRUMBLED FETA CHEESE

SEA SALT

FRESHLY GROUND BLACK PEPPER

Optional Add-ins

HAMBURGER BUNS, FOR SERVING

BACON, COOKED

CARAMELIZED ONIONS

1. In a large cast-iron skillet, heat the olive oil over medium-high heat. Add the garlic and sauté for about 30 seconds.

2. Add the spinach and cook for 1 to 2 minutes, stirring occasionally, until the spinach is wilted. Transfer to a colander and press to remove excess liquid.

3. In a large bowl, add the cooked spinach, ground turkey, and feta cheese, mixing until well combined.

4. Form the mixture into two patties, and season generously with salt and pepper.

5. Heat the cast-iron skillet to medium-high heat. Grill the patties for about 12 minutes, flipping halfway through. The burger patties should be browned on the outside and fully cooked on the inside.

CHICKEN *and* VEGGIE SKEWERS

SERVES 2 • PREP TIME 10 minutes • COOK TIME 15 minutes

The Mediterranean-inspired flavors of these skewers are perfect on a hot summer evening. Turn on the grill and relax after work with your loved one. Serve over a bed of rice or with a fresh side salad. We like to eat them right off the grill and use tzatziki sauce for dipping!

1 TEASPOON PAPRIKA

½ TEASPOON DRIED THYME

SEA SALT

FRESHLY GROUND BLACK PEPPER

½ POUND CHICKEN BREAST, CUT INTO
    1-INCH CUBES

1 CUP CHERRY TOMATOES

1 ZUCCHINI, SLICED

1. Heat the grill to medium.

2. In a small bowl, add the paprika, dried thyme, salt, and pepper. Mix until well combined and generously coat the chicken.

3. Thread the seasoned chicken, tomatoes, and zucchini onto skewers.

4. Place on the grill and cook for 12 to 15 minutes, turning occasionally, until fully cooked.

INGREDIENT SWAP: If you don't have cherry tomatoes or zucchini on hand, you can customize your skewers with whatever veggies you do have. One of my other favorite combinations is onion, pepper, and pineapple.

8

DESSERTS

Peach Crisp **124**

Chocolate Fondue for Two **125**

Mango-Lime Sorbet **126**

Very Berry Frozen Yogurt **127**

Vanilla Bean–Banana Ice Cream **128**

Chocolate Mousse **129**

Flourless Chocolate Cake **130**

Chocolate-Covered Strawberries **131**

Strawberries with Lime Zest and Honey **132**

Chocolate–Chia Seed Pudding **133**

CHOCOLATE–CHIA SEED PUDDING (OPPOSITE), PAGE 133

PEACH CRISP

SERVES 2 • PREP TIME 10 minutes • COOK TIME 10 minutes

Fruit crisps are usually made for a large crowd, but this sized-down crisp is made for two and is especially perfect in the summer when peaches are at their peak. The delicate sweetness of the peaches contrasts beautifully with the buttery, crispy topping. So how do you make something this perfect even better? Add a dollop of fresh whipped cream or a scoop of vanilla ice cream on top.

½ TABLESPOON COCONUT OIL
1 PEACH, CORED AND SLICED
¼ CUP ALMOND FLOUR
2 TABLESPOONS BUTTER
½ TABLESPOON HONEY
½ TEASPOON GROUND CINNAMON
SEA SALT

Optional Add-ins
WHIPPED CREAM
VANILLA ICE CREAM

1. Preheat oven to 350°F.

2. Lightly grease two ramekins with the coconut oil. Divide the peach slices between ramekins.

3. In a small bowl, combine the almond flour, butter, honey, and cinnamon until the mixture becomes crumbly. Spread the mixture evenly on top of the peaches, and sprinkle with a pinch of salt.

4. Place the ramekins on a sheet pan and bake for 10 minutes, or until the crumble turns golden brown.

SEASONAL SWAP: When peaches are no longer in season, swap them for another stone fruit or fresh berries.

CHOCOLATE FONDUE *for* TWO

SERVES 2 • PREP TIME 5 minutes • COOK TIME 2 minutes

Chocolate fondue is the perfect way to end a weeknight meal because it is easy to throw together and fun to eat. We like to dip fruit in ours, but if you have pretzels, marshmallows, or even leftover brownies on hand, they will work well too. After all, there is no such thing as too much chocolate! When serving the fondue, place the hot saucepan on a kitchen towel to keep it from damaging your table.

¾ CUP FULL-FAT COCONUT MILK

8 OUNCES DARK CHOCOLATE, ROUGHLY CHOPPED

SEA SALT

6 STRAWBERRIES

1 BANANA, SLICED

1 APPLE, SLICED

1. In a small nonstick saucepan, heat the coconut milk over low heat, whisking often, until a few bubbles break the surface, forming a gentle simmer.

2. Add the chocolate, and whisk until it melts and the mixture thickens. Sprinkle with a pinch of sea salt. Remove from the heat.

3. Arrange the strawberries, banana, and apple on a plate. Serve with the fondue.

DID YOU KNOW? If you serve the fondue right out of the saucepan, it is easy to reheat as needed by returning the saucepan to the stove over low heat. When reheating, be sure to whisk constantly to prevent the bottom from burning.

MANGO-LIME SORBET

SERVES 2 • PREP TIME 10 minutes

Mango is naturally sweet and creamy, making it the perfect base for this creamy sorbet. The flavors of the coconut milk and lime juice combine to make this an incredibly refreshing dessert. Close your eyes and this sorbet will transport you to a tropical island. If you try hard enough, you might even smell the ocean breeze and feel the sun on your face!

1½ CUP FROZEN MANGO
½ CUP FULL-FAT COCONUT MILK
1 TABLESPOON LIME JUICE

1. In a high-speed blender or food processor, combine the mango, coconut milk, and lime juice. Blend until thick and smooth, scraping down the sides of the blender if needed.

2. Divide the sorbet into two bowls. Serve immediately.

INGREDIENT SWAP: I love the tropical flavor that the coconut milk gives this recipe, but if you don't have coconut milk on hand, you can substitute it with any milk of your choice.

VERY BERRY FROZEN YOGURT

SERVES 2 • PREP TIME 10 minutes

There are a handful of trendy frozen yogurt shops a short walk from our apartment, but why waste your time and money going out when you can make frozen yogurt at home? Frozen berries are full of flavor, while a frozen banana and Greek yogurt keep this version smooth and creamy. Do you like to pile on the toppings? Add chocolate chips, fresh fruit, and whatever else you have on hand.

1 FROZEN BANANA, PEELED AND SLICED
1 CUP FROZEN MIXED BERRIES
½ CUP ALMOND MILK
¼ CUP PLAIN GREEK YOGURT

1. In a high-speed blender or food processor, combine the banana, mixed berries, almond milk, and Greek yogurt. Blend until thick and smooth, scraping down the sides of the blender if needed.

2. Divide the frozen yogurt into two bowls. Serve immediately.

DID YOU KNOW? If you prefer the texture of hard ice cream over the soft-serve texture achieved here, pour the mixture into a small loaf pan after processing and freeze for one hour, or until solid.

VANILLA BEAN-BANANA ICE CREAM

SERVES 2 • PREP TIME 10 minutes

When I first learned that you could turn frozen bananas into ice cream, no bananas in our house were safe. The second we brought a bunch of bananas home from the market, I would cut them up and toss them in the freezer. I made a different flavor of banana ice cream almost every night of the week. This recipe is one of my favorites!

3 FROZEN BANANAS, PEELED AND SLICED
¼ CUP ALMOND MILK
1 TEASPOON VANILLA BEAN PASTE

1. In a high-speed blender or food processor, combine the bananas, almond milk, and vanilla bean paste. Blend until thick and smooth, scraping down the sides of the blender if needed.

2. Divide the ice cream into two bowls. Serve immediately.

INGREDIENT SWAP: This recipe is easy to customize. For example, instead of the vanilla you can use 1 tablespoon of cocoa powder or peanut butter to turn this into a recipe for peanut butter and chocolate banana ice cream!

CHOCOLATE MOUSSE

SERVES 2 • PREP TIME 5 minutes

I am a sucker for chocolate mousse. If it's on the menu at a restaurant, you can be sure I'm ordering it. I used to think it was difficult to make at home and was too intimidated to try, but now I regularly make my own homemade mousse and whipped cream. All it takes is five minutes and a few simple ingredients. I like to use coconut cream (the solids from coconut milk) because of its flavor, but you can use heavy whipping cream if you prefer.

1 (13½-OUNCE) CAN FULL-FAT COCONUT
    MILK, CHILLED
1 TABLESPOON HONEY
1 TABLESPOON COCOA POWDER
1 TEASPOON VANILLA EXTRACT

1. Take the chilled can of coconut milk out of the fridge. Open the can and pour out the liquid, reserving the hardened cream.

2. Scoop the hardened coconut cream into a bowl, and use an electric hand mixer to whip it.

3. Add the honey, cocoa powder, and vanilla extract to the coconut cream, and whip it again until smooth and creamy.

4. Divide the mousse into two bowls. Serve immediately.

FLOURLESS CHOCOLATE CAKE

SERVES 2 • PREP TIME 10 minutes • COOK TIME 20 minutes

Julien and I both prefer ice cream over cake, but this chocolate cake is a very special exception. Rich and decadent, this dessert is a far cry from its light and fluffy namesake. It's perfect for a special occasion, or for when you're just craving a super chocolaty treat.

2 OUNCES DARK CHOCOLATE
½ CUP BUTTER
2 TABLESPOONS COCOA POWDER
1 EGG, PLUS 1 EGG YOLK
¼ CUP HONEY

Optional Add-ins
FRESH BERRIES

1. Preheat the oven to 375°F.

2. In a microwave safe bowl, combine the dark chocolate and butter. Microwave for 2 to 3 minutes, stirring frequently, until completely smooth.

3. Add the cocoa powder, eggs, and honey. Mix well until a smooth batter forms.

4. Gently pour the batter into a lightly greased 4-inch springform pan. Smooth the top using the back of a spoon or spatula.

5. Bake for 15 to 20 minutes, or until the center looks firm.

CHOCOLATE-COVERED STRAWBERRIES

SERVES 2 • PREP TIME 15 minutes • COOK TIME 2 minutes

Chocolate-covered strawberries are synonymous with romance, so I couldn't write a cookbook called Weeknight Cooking for Two *without including them. Keep this treat simple, or for an extra flair sprinkle shredded coconut, chocolate chips, or chopped nuts over the strawberries after dipping them in chocolate. Turn up the romance and serve with your favorite glass of champagne or sparkling wine.*

6 OUNCES DARK CHOCOLATE
½ TABLESPOON COCONUT OIL
6 LARGE STRAWBERRIES

Optional Add-ins
FINELY SHREDDED COCONUT
MINI CHOCOLATE CHIPS
CRUSHED NUTS

1. In a microwave-safe bowl, add the dark chocolate and coconut oil. Microwave for 2 minutes, stirring frequently. Repeat until completely smooth.

2. Hold the top of 1 strawberry, dip it into the chocolate, and swirl to coat evenly. Remove the strawberry from the chocolate and gently shake it to remove excess chocolate.

3. Place the chocolate-covered strawberry on a sheet pan lined with parchment paper. Repeat with the remaining strawberries.

4. Place the sheet pan in the fridge until the chocolate coating is set and dry to the touch.

INGREDIENT SWAP: You can use this chocolate-covering technique on other fruits, pretzels, nuts, and more!

STRAWBERRIES *with* LIME ZEST *and* HONEY

SERVES 2 • PREP TIME 5 minutes • COOK TIME 2 minutes

This is one of my favorite desserts on a hot summer night. It's sweet and refreshing, making it a perfect way to end a meal. Enjoy these strawberries on their own, or use them to top a scoop of ice cream or a slice of pound cake.

2 TABLESPOONS HONEY

½ TABLESPOON LIME JUICE

6 STRAWBERRIES, HALVED

½ TEASPOON LIME ZEST

1. In a small saucepan, over medium-high heat, bring the honey and lime juice to a boil. Remove from the heat and stir.

2. Pour the honey mixture over the strawberries and sprinkle with the lime zest.

CHOCOLATE-CHIA SEED PUDDING

SERVES 2 • PREP TIME 5 minutes

The best desserts are those you can make in advance and taste better with time. This chia pudding is the perfect dessert because it is rich and filling without being too heavy. The best part is that as the chia seeds expand over time, the pudding gets thicker and even more delicious. Make a big batch on Sunday night for dessert throughout the week. You can even swap the cocoa for strawberries, peanut butter, or matcha for a different flavor.

¼ CUP COCOA POWDER

½ CUP CHIA SEEDS

¼ CUP MAPLE SYRUP

2 CUPS ALMOND MILK

SEA SALT

¼ CUP BLUEBERRIES

Optional Add-ins

½ TEASPOON VANILLA EXTRACT

¼ TEASPOON GROUND CINNAMON

1. In a medium bowl, combine the cocoa powder, chia seeds, maple syrup, and almond milk. Add a pinch of sea salt, and whisk until well combined and the cocoa powder has dissolved.

2. Divide the pudding into two jars, cover, and place in the refrigerator for about 20 minutes or until the pudding reaches desired consistency.

3. Top with the blueberries and serve.

DID YOU KNOW? This recipe is easy to assemble in advance. The longer you let the pudding rest in the fridge, the thicker it will become.

the dirty dozen &
the clean fifteen

A nonprofit and environmental watchdog organization called the Environmental Working Group (EWG) looks at data supplied by the US Department of Agriculture (USDA) and the Food and Drug Administration (FDA) about pesticide residues. Each year it compiles a list of the lowest and highest pesticide loads found in commercial crops. You can use these lists to decide which fruits and vegetables to buy organic to minimize your exposure to pesticides and which produce is considered safe enough to buy conventionally. This does not mean they are pesticide-free, though, so wash these fruits and vegetables thoroughly.

THE DIRTY DOZEN

- Apples
- Celery
- Cherry tomatoes
- Cucumbers
- Grapes
- Nectarines (imported)
- Peaches
- Potatoes
- Snap peas (imported)
- Spinach
- Strawberries
- Sweet bell peppers

Kale/Collard greens & Hot peppers*

THE CLEAN FIFTEEN

- Asparagus
- Avocados
- Cabbage
- Cantaloupes (domestic)
- Cauliflower
- Eggplants
- Grapefruit
- Kiwis
- Mangoes
- Onions
- Papayas
- Pineapples
- Sweet corn
- Sweet peas (frozen)
- Sweet potatoes

*In addition to the Dirty Dozen, the EWG added two produce items contaminated with highly toxic organo-phosphate insecticides.

conversion tables

VOLUME EQUIVALENTS (LIQUID)

US STANDARD	US STANDARD (OUNCES)	METRIC (APPROXIMATE)
2 tablespoons	1 fl. oz.	30 mL
¼ cup	2 fl. oz.	60 mL
½ cup	4 fl. oz.	120 mL
1 cup	8 fl. oz.	240 mL
1½ cups	12 fl. oz.	355 mL
2 cups or 1 pint	16 fl. oz.	475 mL
4 cups or 1 quart	32 fl. oz.	1 L
1 gallon	128 fl. oz.	4 L

OVEN TEMPERATURES

FAHRENHEIT (F)	CELSIUS (C) (APPROXIMATE)
250°F	120°C
300°F	150°C
325°F	165°C
350°F	180°C
375°F	190°C
400°F	200°C
425°F	220°C
450°F	230°C

VOLUME EQUIVALENTS (DRY)

US STANDARD	METRIC (APPROXIMATE)
⅛ teaspoon	0.5 mL
¼ teaspoon	1 mL
½ teaspoon	2 mL
¾ teaspoon	4 mL
1 teaspoon	5 mL
1 tablespoon	15 mL
¼ cup	59 mL
⅓ cup	79 mL
½ cup	118 mL
⅔ cup	156 mL
¾ cup	177 mL
1 cup	235 mL
2 cups or 1 pint	475 mL
3 cups	700 mL
4 cups or 1 quart	1 L
½ gallon	2 L
1 gallon	4 L

WEIGHT EQUIVALENTS

US STANDARD	METRIC (APPROXIMATE)
½ ounce	15 g
1 ounce	30 g
2 ounces	60 g
4 ounces	115 g
8 ounces	225 g
12 ounces	340 g
16 ounces or 1 pound	455 g

dietary preference cheat sheet

DAIRY FREE

BREAKFAST FOR DINNER
Shakshuka, 16
Baked Eggs in Mushroom Cups, 17
Sweet Potato Hash with
    Baked Eggs, 18
Brussels Sprouts and Bacon
    Hash, 19
Mediterranean Veggie Frittata, 20
Mushroom and Scallion Frittata, 21
Southwest Breakfast Scramble, 23
Banana Pancakes, 25

SALADS
Classic Chopped Salad, 28
Shredded Brussels Sprouts and
    Quinoa Salad, 29
Roasted Harvest Veggie Salad, 30
Apple-and-Walnut Spinach
    Salad, 31
Chicken BLT Salad, 33
Fall Cobb Salad, 34
Chinese Chicken Salad, 36
Kale and Quinoa Salad, 37

SOUPS & SANDWICHES
Cream of Broccoli Soup, 40
Wild Mushroom Soup, 42
Pumpkin-Coconut Soup, 43
Black Bean Soup, 44
White Chicken Chili, 45
Creamy Vegetable Soup, 47
Carrot and Ginger Soup, 48
Chicken Club Wrap, 49
Tuna and Avocado Wrap, 50
Chicken Salad Lettuce Wrap, 51
Eggplant, Avocado, and Bacon
    Roll-up, 52
Classic Burger, 54

VEGETARIAN
Roasted Veggie Kabobs, 58
Grilled Zucchini Tacos, 59
Simple Sheet-Pan Veggies, 60
Buddha Bowl, 61
Roasted Eggplant with Brussels
    Sprouts Salad, 63
Mexican Brown Rice, 65
Butternut Squash Curry, 68
Sweet Potato Gnocchi, 71

SEAFOOD
Orange Shrimp with Green Beans
    en Papillote, 76
Grilled Halibut and Rice, 77
Roasted Honey-Garlic Salmon, 78
Lemon Risotto and Shrimp, 79
Mediterranean Baked Salmon, 80
Prosciutto-Wrapped Scallops, 82
Sheet-Pan Salmon with
    Mushrooms and Peppers, 84
Mussels and Chorizo in Red Wine
    Sauce, 85

MEAT
Thirty-Minute Meatballs, 88
Simple Beef Chili, 89
Pork Fried Rice, 90
Beef and Broccoli, 91
Mushroom Bolognese, 92
Sheet-Pan Steak and Veggies, 93
Beef Tenderloin with Cauliflower
    and Kale, 96
Sausage and Roasted Veggies, 97
Tangy Orange Lamb Chops, 100
Open-Faced Bacon and
    Brussels Burger, 101
Beef and Tomato Skewers, 102

POULTRY

Simple Chicken Piccata, 106
Chicken and Broccoli, 107
Cilantro-Lime Chicken, 109
Asian Chicken Lettuce Wraps, 110
Rice Bowl with Thai-Basil
  Chicken, 111
Lemon-Rosemary Chicken with
  Broccolini, 112
Shredded Chicken Tacos, 113

Chicken Thighs with Tomatoes
  and Asparagus, 116
Easy Chicken Marsala, 117
Herbed Chicken and
  Potatoes, 118
Chicken and Veggie Skewers, 121

DESSERTS

Chocolate Fondue for Two, 125
Mango-Lime Sorbet, 126

Vanilla Bean–Banana Ice
  Cream, 128
Chocolate Mousse, 129
Chocolate-Covered
  Strawberries, 131
Strawberries with Lime Zest
  and Honey, 132
Chocolate–Chia Seed
  Pudding, 133

GLUTEN FREE

BREAKFAST FOR DINNER

Shakshuka, 16
Baked Eggs in Mushroom
  Cups, 17
Sweet Potato Hash with
  Baked Eggs, 18
Brussels Sprouts and Bacon
  Hash, 19
Mediterranean Veggie Frittata, 20
Mushroom and Scallion
  Frittata, 21
Poached Egg over Creamy Polenta
  with Sautéed Spinach, 22
Southwest Breakfast Scramble, 23
Steak and Eggs, 24
Banana Pancakes, 25

SALADS

Classic Chopped Salad, 28
Shredded Brussels Sprouts and
  Quinoa Salad, 29
Roasted Harvest Veggie Salad, 30
Apple-and-Walnut Spinach
  Salad, 31

Grilled Romaine and Chicken
  Caesar Salad, 32
Chicken BLT Salad, 33
Fall Cobb Salad, 34
Traditional Greek Salad, 35
Chinese Chicken Salad, 36
Kale and Quinoa Salad, 37

SOUPS & SANDWICHES

Cream of Broccoli Soup, 40
Creamy Tomato Soup, 41
Wild Mushroom Soup, 42
Pumpkin-Coconut Soup, 43
Black Bean Soup, 44
White Chicken Chili, 45
Cauliflower and Celeriac Soup, 46
Creamy Vegetable Soup, 47
Carrot and Ginger Soup, 48
Chicken Club Wrap, 49
Tuna and Avocado Wrap, 50
Chicken Salad Lettuce Wrap, 51
Eggplant, Avocado, and Bacon
  Roll-up, 52
Portobello Philly Cheesesteak, 53

VEGETARIAN

Roasted Veggie Kabobs, 58
Grilled Zucchini Tacos, 59
Simple Sheet-Pan Veggies, 60
Buddha Bowl, 61
Sweet Potato Stuffed with
  Spinach and Feta, 62
Roasted Eggplant with Brussels
  Sprouts Salad, 63
Spaghetti Squash and Pesto, 64
Mexican Brown Rice, 65
Cauliflower Pizza, 66
Mushroom Risotto, 67
Butternut Squash Curry, 68
Cheesy Polenta with Brussels
  Sprouts and Mushrooms, 69
Mushrooms Stuffed with Cheese
  and Herbs, 70
Sweet Potato Gnocchi, 71
Simple Eggplant Lasagna, 72

SEAFOOD

Orange Shrimp with Green Beans en Papillote, 76

Grilled Halibut and Rice, 77

Roasted Honey-Garlic Salmon, 78

Lemon Risotto and Shrimp, 79

Mediterranean Baked Salmon, 80

Simple Shrimp Scampi, 81

Prosciutto-Wrapped Scallops, 82

Pan-Seared Scallops in a White Wine Sauce, 83

Sheet-Pan Salmon with Mushrooms and Peppers, 84

Mussels and Chorizo in Red Wine Sauce, 85

MEAT

Thirty-Minute Meatballs, 88

Simple Beef Chili, 89

Pork Fried Rice, 90

Beef and Broccoli, 91

Mushroom Bolognese, 92

Sheet-Pan Steak and Veggies, 93

Maple Pork and Pears, 94

Steak Frites, 95

Beef Tenderloin with Cauliflower and Kale, 96

Sausage and Roasted Veggies, 97

Stuffed Zucchini Boats, 98

Southwest Stuffed Peppers, 99

Tangy Orange Lamb Chops, 100

Open-Faced Bacon and Brussels Burger, 101

Beef and Tomato Skewers, 102

POULTRY

Simple Chicken Piccata, 106

Chicken and Broccoli, 107

Chicken Tikka Masala, 108

Cilantro-Lime Chicken, 109

Asian Chicken Lettuce Wraps, 110

Rice Bowl with Thai-Basil Chicken, 111

Lemon-Rosemary Chicken with Broccolini, 112

Shredded Chicken Tacos, 113

Potato Stuffed with Broccoli, Cheddar, and Chicken, 114

Chicken Thighs with Tomatoes and Asparagus, 116

Easy Chicken Marsala, 117

Herbed Chicken and Potatoes, 118

Turkey Steaks with Mushrooms, 119

Spinach-Turkey Burger, 120

Chicken and Veggie Skewers, 121

DESSERTS

Peach Crisp, 124

Chocolate Fondue for Two, 125

Mango-Lime Sorbet, 126

Very Berry Frozen Yogurt, 127

Vanilla Bean–Banana Ice Cream, 128

Chocolate Mousse, 129

Flourless Chocolate Cake, 130

Chocolate-Covered Strawberries, 131

Strawberries with Lime Zest and Honey, 132

Chocolate–Chia Seed Pudding, 133

PALEO

BREAKFAST FOR DINNER

Shakshuka, 16

Baked Eggs in Mushroom Cups, 17

Sweet Potato Hash with Baked Eggs, 18

Brussels Sprouts and Bacon Hash, 19

Mediterranean Veggie Frittata, 20

Mushroom and Scallion Frittata, 21

Steak and Eggs, 24

Banana Pancakes, 25

SALADS

Classic Chopped Salad, 28

Roasted Harvest Veggie Salad, 30

Apple-and-Walnut Spinach Salad, 31

Chicken BLT Salad, 33

Fall Cobb Salad, 34

SOUPS & SANDWICHES

Cream of Broccoli Soup, 40
Creamy Tomato Soup, 41
Wild Mushroom Soup, 42
Pumpkin-Coconut Soup, 43
Cauliflower and Celeriac Soup, 46
Creamy Vegetable Soup, 47
Carrot and Ginger Soup, 48
Chicken Club Wrap, 49
Tuna and Avocado Wrap, 50
Chicken Salad Lettuce Wrap, 51
Eggplant, Avocado, and Bacon
    Roll-up, 52

VEGETARIAN

Roasted Veggie Kabobs, 58
Simple Sheet-Pan Veggies, 60
Roasted Eggplant with Brussels
    Sprouts Salad, 63
Butternut Squash Curry, 68
Sweet Potato Gnocchi, 71

SEAFOOD

Orange Shrimp with Green Beans
    en Papillote, 76
Roasted Honey-Garlic
    Salmon, 78
Mediterranean Baked Salmon, 80
Simple Shrimp Scampi, 81
Prosciutto-Wrapped Scallops, 82
Pan-Seared Scallops in a White
    Wine Sauce, 83
Sheet-Pan Salmon with
    Mushrooms and Peppers, 84
Mussels and Chorizo in Red
    Wine Sauce, 85

MEAT

Thirty-Minute Meatballs, 88
Beef and Broccoli, 91
Mushroom Bolognese, 92
Sheet-Pan Steak and Veggies, 93
Maple Pork and Pears, 94
Steak Frites, 95
Beef Tenderloin with Cauliflower
    and Kale, 96
Sausage and Roasted Veggies, 97
Tangy Orange Lamb Chops, 100
Open-Faced Bacon and Brussels
    Burger, 101
Beef and Tomato Skewers, 102

POULTRY

Simple Chicken Piccata, 106
Chicken and Broccoli, 107
Cilantro-Lime Chicken, 109
Asian Chicken Lettuce Wraps, 110
Lemon-Rosemary Chicken
    with Broccolini, 112
Chicken Thighs with Tomatoes
    and Asparagus, 116
Easy Chicken Marsala, 117
Herbed Chicken and Potatoes, 118
Turkey Steaks with
    Mushrooms, 119
Chicken and Veggie Skewers, 121

DESSERTS

Peach Crisp, 124
Chocolate Fondue for Two, 125
Mango-Lime Sorbet, 126
Vanilla Bean–Banana Ice
    Cream, 128
Chocolate Mousse, 129
Flourless Chocolate Cake, 130
Chocolate-Covered
    Strawberries, 131
Strawberries with Lime Zest
    and Honey, 132
Chocolate–Chia Seed
    Pudding, 133

VEGETARIAN

BREAKFAST FOR DINNER

Shakshuka, 16
Sweet Potato Hash with
    Baked Eggs, 18
Mediterranean Veggie Frittata, 20

Mushroom and Scallion
    Frittata, 21
Poached Egg over Creamy
    Polenta with Sautéed
    Spinach, 22

Southwest Breakfast
    Scramble, 23
Banana Pancakes, 25

SALADS

Classic Chopped Salad, 28

Shredded Brussels Sprouts and
   Quinoa Salad, 29

Roasted Harvest Veggie Salad, 30

Apple-and-Walnut Spinach
   Salad, 31

Traditional Greek Salad, 35

Kale and Quinoa Salad, 37

SOUPS & SANDWICHES

Cream of Broccoli Soup, 40

Creamy Tomato Soup, 41

Pumpkin-Coconut Soup, 43

Creamy Vegetable Soup, 47

Carrot and Ginger Soup, 48

VEGETARIAN

Roasted Veggie Kabobs, 58

Grilled Zucchini Tacos, 59

Simple Sheet-Pan Veggies, 60

Buddha Bowl, 61

Sweet Potato Stuffed with
   Spinach and Feta, 62

Roasted Eggplant with Brussels
   Sprouts Salad, 63

Spaghetti Squash and Pesto, 64

Mexican Brown Rice, 65

Cauliflower Pizza, 66

Mushroom Risotto, 67

Butternut Squash Curry, 68

Cheesy Polenta with Brussels
   Sprouts and Mushrooms, 69

Mushrooms Stuffed with Cheese
   and Herbs, 70

Sweet Potato Gnocchi, 71

Simple Eggplant Lasagna, 72

DESSERTS

Peach Crisp, 124

Chocolate Fondue for Two, 125

Mango-Lime Sorbet, 126

Very Berry Frozen Yogurt, 127

Vanilla Bean–Banana Ice
   Cream, 128

Chocolate Mousse, 129

Flourless Chocolate Cake, 130

Chocolate-Covered
   Strawberries, 131

Strawberries with Lime Zest
   and Honey, 132

Chocolate–Chia Seed Pudding,
   133

VEGAN

SALADS

Classic Chopped Salad, 28

Shredded Brussels Sprouts and
   Quinoa Salad, 29

Roasted Harvest Veggie Salad, 30

Apple-and-Walnut Spinach
   Salad, 31

Kale and Quinoa Salad, 37

SOUPS & SANDWICHES

Cream of Broccoli Soup, 40

Pumpkin-Coconut Soup, 43

Creamy Vegetable Soup, 47

Carrot and Ginger Soup, 48

VEGETARIAN

Roasted Veggie Kabobs, 58

Grilled Zucchini Tacos, 59

Simple Sheet-Pan Veggies, 60

Buddha Bowl, 61

Mexican Brown Rice, 65

Butternut Squash Curry, 68

Sweet Potato Gnocchi, 71

DESSERTS

Chocolate Fondue for Two, 125

Mango-Lime Sorbet, 126

Vanilla Bean–Banana Ice
   Cream, 128

Chocolate-Covered
   Strawberries, 131

Chocolate–Chia Seed Pudding,
   133

recipe index

A

Apple-and-Walnut Spinach Salad, 31
Asian Chicken Lettuce Wraps, 110

B

Baked Eggs in Mushroom Cups, 17
Banana Pancakes, 25
Beef and Broccoli, 91
Beef and Tomato Skewers, 102
Beef Tenderloin with Cauliflower
    and Kale, 96
Black Bean Soup, 44
Brussels Sprouts and Bacon Hash, 19
Buddha Bowl, 61
Butternut Squash Curry, 68

C

Caesar Dressing, 45
Carrot and Ginger Soup, 48
Cauliflower and Celeriac Soup, 46
Cauliflower Pizza, 66
Cheesy Polenta with Brussels
    Sprouts and Mushrooms, 69
Chicken and Broccoli, 107
Chicken and Veggie Skewers, 121
Chicken BLT Salad, 33
Chicken Club Wrap, 49
Chicken Salad Lettuce Wrap, 51
Chicken Thighs with Tomatoes
    and Asparagus, 116
Chicken Tikka Masala, 108
Chinese Chicken Salad, 36
Chocolate–Chia Seed Pudding, 133
Chocolate-Covered Strawberries, 131
Chocolate Fondue for Two, 125
Chocolate Mousse, 129
Cilantro-Lime Chicken, 109
Classic Burger, 54

Classic Chopped Salad, 28
Cream of Broccoli Soup, 40
Creamy Tomato Soup, 41
Creamy Vegetable Soup, 47

E

Easy Chicken Marsala, 117
Eggplant, Avocado, and
    Bacon Roll-up, 52

F

Fall Cobb Salad, 34
Flourless Chocolate Cake, 130

G

Grilled Halibut and Rice, 77
Grilled Romaine and Chicken
    Caesar Salad, 32
Grilled Zucchini Tacos, 59

H

Herbed Chicken and Potatoes, 118

K

Kale and Quinoa Salad, 37

L

Lemon Risotto and Shrimp, 79
Lemon-Rosemary Chicken
    with Broccolini, 112

M

Mango-Lime Sorbet, 126
Maple Pork and Pears, 94
Mediterranean Baked Salmon, 80
Mediterranean Veggie Frittata, 20

Mexican Brown Rice, 65
Mushroom and Scallion Frittata, 21
Mushroom Bolognese, 92
Mushroom Risotto, 67
Mushrooms Stuffed with
    Cheese and Herbs, 70
Mussels and Chorizo in Red
    Wine Sauce, 85

O

Open-Faced Bacon and
    Brussels Burger, 101
Orange Shrimp with Green
    Beans en Papillote, 76

P

Pan-Seared Scallops in a
    White Wine Sauce, 83
Peach Crisp, 124
Poached Egg over Creamy Polenta
    with Sautéed Spinach, 22
Pork Fried Rice, 90
Portobello Philly Cheesesteak, 53
Potato Stuffed with Broccoli,
    Cheddar, and Chicken, 114–115
Prosciutto-Wrapped Scallops, 82
Pumpkin-Coconut Soup, 43

R

Rice Bowl with Thai-Basil
    Chicken, 111
Roasted Eggplant with Brussels
    Sprouts Salad, 63
Roasted Harvest Veggie Salad, 30
Roasted Honey-Garlic Salmon, 78
Roasted Veggie Kabobs, 58

S

Sausage and Roasted Veggies, 97
Shakshuka, 16
Sheet-Pan Salmon with Mushrooms
    and Peppers, 84
Sheet-Pan Steak and Veggies, 93
Shredded Brussels Sprouts
    and Quinoa Salad, 29
Shredded Chicken Tacos, 113
Simple Beef Chili, 89
Simple Chicken Piccata, 106
Simple Eggplant Lasagna, 72
Simple Sheet-Pan Veggies, 60
Simple Shrimp Scampi, 81

Southwest Breakfast Scramble, 23
Southwest Stuffed Peppers, 99
Spaghetti Squash and Pesto, 64
Spinach-Turkey Burger, 120
Steak and Eggs, 24
Steak Frites, 95
Strawberries with Lime Zest
    and Honey, 132
Stuffed Zucchini Boats, 98
Sweet Potato Gnocchi, 71
Sweet Potato Hash with
    Baked Eggs, 18
Sweet Potato Stuffed with
    Spinach and Feta, 62

T

Tangy Orange Lamb Chops, 100
Thirty-Minute Meatballs, 88
Traditional Greek Salad, 35
Tuna and Avocado Wrap, 50
Turkey Steaks with Mushrooms, 119

V

Vanilla Bean–Banana Ice Cream, 128
Very Berry Frozen Yogurt, 127

W

White Chicken Chili, 45
Wild Mushroom Soup, 42

index

A

Almond flour
  Banana Pancakes, 25
  Peach Crisp, 124
  Sweet Potato Gnocchi, 71
  Thirty-Minute Meatballs, 88
Almond milk
  Chocolate–Chia Seed Pudding, 133
  Very Berry Frozen Yogurt, 127
Apples
  Apple-and-Walnut
    Spinach Salad, 31
  Brussels Sprouts and
    Bacon Hash, 19
  Chocolate Fondue for Two, 125
  Classic Chopped Salad, 28
  Fall Cobb Salad, 34
Arugula
  Eggplant, Avocado, and
    Bacon Roll-up, 52
Asparagus
  Buddha Bowl, 61
  Chicken Thighs with Tomatoes
    and Asparagus, 116
  Sheet-Pan Steak and Veggies, 93
Avocados
  Cilantro-Lime Chicken, 109
  Classic Chopped Salad, 28
  Eggplant, Avocado, and
    Bacon Roll-Up, 52
  Kale and Quinoa Salad, 37
  Tuna and Avocado Wrap, 50

B

Bacon
  Brussels Sprouts and
    Bacon Hash, 19
  Chicken BLT Salad, 33
  Chicken Club Wrap, 49
  Eggplant, Avocado, and
    Bacon Roll-up, 52
  Fall Cobb Salad, 34
  Open-Faced Bacon and
    Brussels Burger, 101
Bananas
  Banana Pancakes, 25
  Chocolate Fondue for Two, 125
  Vanilla Bean–Banana
    Ice Cream, 128
  Very Berry Frozen Yogurt, 127
Basil
  Rice Bowl with Thai-
    Basil Chicken, 111
  Spaghetti Squash and Pesto, 64
Beans and legumes. See specific
Beef
  Beef and Broccoli, 91
  Beef and Tomato Skewers, 102
  Beef Tenderloin with
    Cauliflower and Kale, 96
  Classic Burger, 54
  Mushroom Bolognese, 92
  Open-Faced Bacon and
    Brussels Burger, 101
  Portobello Philly Cheesesteak, 53
  Sheet-Pan Steak and Veggies, 93
  Simple Beef Chili, 89
  Southwest Stuffed Peppers, 99
  Steak and Eggs, 24
  Steak Frites, 95
  Stuffed Zucchini Boats, 98
  Thirty-Minute Meatballs, 88
Bell peppers
  Shakshuka, 16
  Sheet-Pan Salmon with
    Mushrooms and Peppers, 84
  Southwest Breakfast Scramble, 23
  Southwest Stuffed Peppers, 99
Berries. See also Strawberries
  Chocolate–Chia Seed Pudding, 133
  Very Berry Frozen Yogurt, 127
Black beans
  Black Bean Soup, 44
  Mexican Brown Rice, 65
  Simple Beef Chili, 89
  Southwest Breakfast Scramble, 23
Broccoli
  Beef and Broccoli, 91
  Chicken and Broccoli, 107
  Cream of Broccoli Soup, 40
  Potato Stuffed with Broccoli,
    Cheddar, and Chicken, 114–115
  Roasted Veggie Kabobs, 58
  Simple Sheet-Pan Veggies, 60
Broccolini
  Lemon-Rosemary Chicken
    with Broccolini, 112
Brussels sprouts
  Brussels Sprouts and
    Bacon Hash, 19
  Cheesy Polenta with Brussels
    Sprouts and Mushrooms, 69
  Open-Faced Bacon and
    Brussels Burger, 101
  Roasted Eggplant with Brussels
    Sprouts Salad, 63
  Roasted Harvest Veggie Salad, 30
  Sausage and Roasted Veggies, 97
  Shredded Brussels Sprouts
    and Quinoa Salad, 29

C

Cabbage
  Chinese Chicken Salad, 36
  Grilled Zucchini Tacos, 59
Cannellini beans

White Chicken Chili, 45

Capers
Simple Chicken Piccata, 106

Carrots
Carrot and Ginger Soup, 48
Chinese Chicken Salad, 36
Creamy Vegetable Soup, 47
Maple Pork and Pears, 94
Simple Sheet-Pan Veggies, 60

Cast-iron skillets, 12

Cauliflower
Beef Tenderloin with
Cauliflower and Kale, 96
Cauliflower and Celeriac Soup, 46
Cauliflower Pizza, 66
Cream of Broccoli Soup, 40

Celeriac
Cauliflower and Celeriac Soup, 46

Celery
Chicken Salad Lettuce Wrap, 51
Creamy Vegetable Soup, 47

Cheddar cheese
Potato Stuffed with Broccoli,
Cheddar, and Chicken, 114–115

Cheese. See also specific
storing, 103

Chia seeds
Chocolate–Chia Seed Pudding, 133

Chicken
Asian Chicken Lettuce Wraps, 110
Chicken and Broccoli, 107
Chicken and Veggie Skewers, 121
Chicken BLT Salad, 33
Chicken Club Wrap, 49
Chicken Salad Lettuce Wrap, 51
Chicken Thighs with Tomatoes
and Asparagus, 116
Chicken Tikka Masala, 108
Chinese Chicken Salad, 36
Cilantro-Lime Chicken, 109
Easy Chicken Marsala, 117
Grilled Romaine and Chicken
Caesar Salad, 32
Herbed Chicken and Potatoes, 118

Lemon-Rosemary Chicken
with Broccolini, 112
Potato Stuffed with Broccoli,
Cheddar, and Chicken, 114–115
Rice Bowl with Thai-
Basil Chicken, 111
Shredded Chicken Tacos, 113
Simple Chicken Piccata, 106
White Chicken Chili, 45

Chocolate. See also Cocoa powder
Chocolate-Covered
Strawberries, 131
Chocolate Fondue for Two, 125
Flourless Chocolate Cake, 130

Cilantro
Cilantro-Lime Chicken, 109
Mediterranean Baked Salmon, 80

Cocoa powder
Chocolate–Chia Seed Pudding, 133
Chocolate Mousse, 129
Flourless Chocolate Cake, 130

Coconut milk
Butternut Squash Curry, 68
Carrot and Ginger Soup, 48
Chicken Tikka Masala, 108
Chocolate Fondue for Two, 125
Chocolate Mousse, 129
Cilantro-Lime Chicken, 109
Cream of Broccoli Soup, 40
Creamy Tomato Soup, 41
Mango-Lime Sorbet, 126
Mediterranean Veggie Frittata, 20
Mushroom and Scallion Frittata, 21
Pumpkin-Coconut Soup, 43
Southwest Breakfast Scramble, 23
Wild Mushroom Soup, 42

Cooking tips, 55

Corn
Mexican Brown Rice, 65

Cranberries
Apple-and-Walnut
Spinach Salad, 31

Cucumbers
Traditional Greek Salad, 35

E

Edamame
Chinese Chicken Salad, 36

Eggplant
Eggplant, Avocado, and
Bacon Roll-up, 52
Roasted Eggplant with Brussels
Sprouts Salad, 63
Simple Eggplant Lasagna, 72

Eggs
Baked Eggs in Mushroom Cups, 17
Chicken BLT Salad, 33
Fall Cobb Salad, 34
Flourless Chocolate Cake, 130
Mediterranean Veggie Frittata, 20
Mushroom and Scallion Frittata, 21
Poached Egg over Creamy Polenta
with Sautéed Spinach, 22
Pork Fried Rice, 90
Southwest Breakfast Scramble, 23
Steak and Eggs, 24
storing, 103
Sweet Potato Hash with
Baked Eggs, 18

Equipment, 12–13

F

Feta cheese
Spinach-Turkey Burger, 120
Sweet Potato Stuffed with
Spinach and Feta, 62
Traditional Greek Salad, 35

Fish. See Halibut; Salmon; Tuna

Food waste, avoiding, 103

Fruits. See specific

G

Garlic
Mediterranean Baked Salmon, 80
Roasted Honey-Garlic Salmon, 78
Simple Shrimp Scampi, 81
storing, 103

Ginger
    Beef and Broccoli, 91
    Butternut Squash Curry, 68
    Carrot and Ginger Soup, 48
    Chicken and Broccoli, 107
    Grilled Halibut and Rice, 77
    Orange Shrimp with Green
       Beans en Papillote, 76
Glass baking dishes, 13
Goat cheese
    Mushrooms Stuffed with
       Cheese and Herbs, 70
Grapes
    Chicken Salad Lettuce Wrap, 51
Greek yogurt
    Chicken Tikka Masala, 108
    Potato Stuffed with Broccoli,
       Cheddar, and Chicken, 114–115
    Very Berry Frozen Yogurt, 127
Green beans
    Orange Shrimp with Green
       Beans en Papillote, 76

H

Halibut
    Grilled Halibut and Rice, 77
Herbs and spices, storing, 103

J

Jalapeños
    Grilled Zucchini Tacos, 59
    Tuna and Avocado Wrap, 50

K

Kale
    Beef Tenderloin with
       Cauliflower and Kale, 96
    Classic Chopped Salad, 28
    Kale and Quinoa Salad, 37

L

Leafy greens. See also Arugula; Kale;
    Lettuce; Radicchio; Spinach

Chicken BLT Salad, 33
Lemons and lemon juice
    Apple-and-Walnut
       Spinach Salad, 31
    Beef Tenderloin with
       Cauliflower and Kale, 96
    Chicken Thighs with Tomatoes
       and Asparagus, 116
    Classic Chopped Salad, 28
    Kale and Quinoa Salad, 37
    Lemon Risotto and Shrimp, 79
    Lemon-Rosemary Chicken
       with Broccolini, 112
    Mediterranean Baked Salmon, 80
    Prosciutto-Wrapped Scallops, 82
    Roasted Eggplant with Brussels
       Sprouts Salad, 63
    Shredded Brussels Sprouts
       and Quinoa Salad, 29
    Simple Chicken Piccata, 106
Lettuce
    Asian Chicken Lettuce Wraps, 110
    Chicken Club Wrap, 49
    Chicken Salad Lettuce Wrap, 51
    Chinese Chicken Salad, 36
    Classic Burger, 54
    Fall Cobb Salad, 34
    Grilled Romaine and Chicken
       Caesar Salad, 32
    Tuna and Avocado Wrap, 50
Limes and lime juice
    Cilantro-Lime Chicken, 109
    Mango-Lime Sorbet, 126
    Strawberries with Lime
       Zest and Honey, 132
    Tuna and Avocado Wrap, 50

M

Mangoes
    Mango-Lime Sorbet, 126
Mayonnaise, 49
Meal prepping and planning, 55, 73
Meat. See also Beef; Pork
    Tangy Orange Lamb Chops, 100

Millet flour
    Sweet Potato Gnocchi, 71
Mozzarella cheese
    Cauliflower Pizza, 66
    Simple Eggplant Lasagna, 72
    Stuffed Zucchini Boats, 98
Mushrooms
    Asian Chicken Lettuce Wraps, 110
    Baked Eggs in Mushroom Cups, 17
    Cheesy Polenta with Brussels
       Sprouts and Mushrooms, 69
    Easy Chicken Marsala, 117
    Mushroom and Scallion Frittata, 21
    Mushroom Bolognese, 92
    Mushroom Risotto, 67
    Mushrooms Stuffed with
       Cheese and Herbs, 70
    Portobello Philly Cheesesteak, 53
    Roasted Harvest Veggie Salad, 30
    Roasted Veggie Kabobs, 58
    Sheet-Pan Salmon with
       Mushrooms and Peppers, 84
    Simple Sheet-Pan Veggies, 60
    storing, 103
    Turkey Steaks with
       Mushrooms, 119
    Wild Mushroom Soup, 42
Mussels
    Mussels and Chorizo in
       Red Wine Sauce, 85

N

Nonstick pans, 12
Nuts and seeds. See also specific
    storing, 103

O

Olives, black
    Mediterranean Veggie Frittata, 20
Olives, Kalamata
    Traditional Greek Salad, 35
Onions
    Classic Burger, 54
    Portobello Philly Cheesesteak, 53

Simple Beef Chili, 89
storing, 103
Thirty-Minute Meatballs, 88
Oranges and orange juice
Grilled Halibut and Rice, 77
Orange Shrimp with Green
Beans en Papillote, 76
Tangy Orange Lamb Chops, 100

P

Pantry staples, 10–11
Parmesan cheese
Cauliflower Pizza, 66
Cheesy Polenta with Brussels
Sprouts and Mushrooms, 69
Grilled Romaine and Chicken
Caesar Salad, 32
Poached Egg over Creamy Polenta
with Sautéed Spinach, 22
Spaghetti Squash and Pesto, 64
Steak Frites, 95
Peaches
Peach Crisp, 124
Pears
Maple Pork and Pears, 94
Pecans
Fall Cobb Salad, 34
Kale and Quinoa Salad, 37
Pepper Jack cheese
Southwest Stuffed Peppers, 99
Pine nuts
Spaghetti Squash and Pesto, 64
Polenta
Cheesy Polenta with Brussels
Sprouts and Mushrooms, 69
Poached Egg over Creamy Polenta
with Sautéed Spinach, 22
Pomegranate seeds
Shredded Brussels Sprouts
and Quinoa Salad, 29
Pork. See also Bacon; Prosciutto
Maple Pork and Pears, 94
Mussels and Chorizo in
Red Wine Sauce, 85

Pork Fried Rice, 90
Sausage and Roasted Veggies, 97
Potatoes. See also Sweet potatoes
Creamy Vegetable Soup, 47
Herbed Chicken and Potatoes, 118
Potato Stuffed with Broccoli,
Cheddar, and Chicken, 114–115
Sheet-Pan Steak and Veggies, 93
Steak Frites, 95
storing, 103
Poultry. See Chicken; Turkey
Prosciutto
Baked Eggs in Mushroom Cups, 17
Prosciutto-Wrapped Scallops, 82
Provolone cheese
Portobello Philly Cheesesteak, 53
Pumpkin
Pumpkin-Coconut Soup, 43

Q

Quinoa
Buddha Bowl, 61
Kale and Quinoa Salad, 37
Shredded Brussels Sprouts
and Quinoa Salad, 29
Southwest Stuffed Peppers, 99

R

Radicchio
Classic Chopped Salad, 28
Red beans
Buddha Bowl, 61
Rice
Grilled Halibut and Rice, 77
Lemon Risotto and Shrimp, 79
Mexican Brown Rice, 65
Mushroom Risotto, 67
Pork Fried Rice, 90
Rice Bowl with Thai-
Basil Chicken, 111
Rosemary
Lemon-Rosemary Chicken
with Broccolini, 112

S

Salmon
Mediterranean Baked Salmon, 80
Roasted Honey-Garlic Salmon, 78
Sheet-Pan Salmon with
Mushrooms and Peppers, 84
Salsa verde, 45
Scallions
Mushroom and Scallion Frittata, 21
Scallops
Pan-Seared Scallops in a
White Wine Sauce, 83
Prosciutto-Wrapped Scallops, 82
Shallots
Beef Tenderloin with
Cauliflower and Kale, 96
Simple Sheet-Pan Veggies, 60
Steak and Eggs, 24
storing, 103
Wild Mushroom Soup, 42
Sheet pans, 12
Shopping tips, 73
Shrimp
Lemon Risotto and Shrimp, 79
Orange Shrimp with Green
Beans en Papillote, 76
Simple Shrimp Scampi, 81
Spinach
Apple-and-Walnut
Spinach Salad, 31
Poached Egg over Creamy Polenta
with Sautéed Spinach, 22
Prosciutto-Wrapped Scallops, 82
Spinach-Turkey Burger, 120
Sweet Potato Stuffed with
Spinach and Feta, 62
Turkey Steaks with
Mushrooms, 119
Squash. See also Zucchini
Butternut Squash Curry, 68
Sausage and Roasted Veggies, 97
Spaghetti Squash and Pesto, 64
storing, 103
Stock pots, 13

Strawberries
    Chocolate-Covered
        Strawberries, 131
    Chocolate Fondue for Two, 125
    Strawberries with Lime
        Zest and Honey, 132
Sweet potatoes
    Buddha Bowl, 61
    Creamy Vegetable Soup, 47
    Roasted Harvest Veggie Salad, 30
    Sweet Potato Gnocchi, 71
    Sweet Potato Hash with
        Baked Eggs, 18
    Sweet Potato Stuffed with
        Spinach and Feta, 62

T

Tahini
    Roasted Harvest Veggie Salad, 30
Tamari
    Asian Chicken Lettuce Wraps, 110
    Beef and Broccoli, 91
    Chicken and Broccoli, 107
    Pork Fried Rice, 90
    Rice Bowl with Thai-
        Basil Chicken, 111
    Roasted Honey-Garlic Salmon, 78
    Sheet-Pan Salmon with
        Mushrooms and Peppers, 84

Tips
    cooking, 55
    shopping, 73
    storing ingredients, 103
Tomatoes
    Beef and Tomato Skewers, 102
    Black Bean Soup, 44
    Butternut Squash Curry, 68
    Chicken and Veggie Skewers, 121
    Chicken BLT Salad, 33
    Chicken Club Wrap, 49
    Chicken Thighs with Tomatoes
        and Asparagus, 116
    Classic Burger, 54
    Creamy Tomato Soup, 41
    Mediterranean Baked Salmon, 80
    Mediterranean Veggie Frittata, 20
    Roasted Veggie Kabobs, 58
    Shakshuka, 16
    Shredded Chicken Tacos, 113
    Simple Beef Chili, 89
    storing, 103
    Traditional Greek Salad, 35
Tuna
    Tuna and Avocado Wrap, 50
Turkey
    Spinach-Turkey Burger, 120
    Turkey Steaks with
        Mushrooms, 119

V

Vegetables. *See also specific*
    Pork Fried Rice, 90

W

Walnuts
    Apple-and-Walnut
        Spinach Salad, 31
    Shredded Brussels Sprouts
        and Quinoa Salad, 29
Wine, Marsala
    Easy Chicken Marsala, 117
Wine, red
    Mussels and Chorizo in
        Red Wine Sauce, 85
Wine, white
    Orange Shrimp with Green
        Beans en Papillote, 76
    Pan-Seared Scallops in a
        White Wine Sauce, 83

Y

Yogurt. *See Greek yogurt*

Z

Zucchini
    Chicken and Veggie Skewers, 121
    Grilled Zucchini Tacos, 59
    Simple Shrimp Scampi, 81
    Stuffed Zucchini Boats, 98

acknowledgments

To Julien, thank you for your unwavering love and support in everything I do. Thank you for encouraging me to take on new challenges and for always having faith in me.

To my mom, thank you for always believing in me and encouraging me to follow my heart and chase my dreams.

To Michael and Nickolas, thank you for being the best brothers a girl could ask for and always being my biggest fans.

To Alex, Maddison, Alex, and Lindsey, thank you for always being up for a new restaurant, trying my new recipes, and inspiring so many of the stories in this book.

To my friends and family, thank you for always eating my kitchen experiments, cheering for me throughout this journey, and for always tagging me in pictures of your re-creations.

To my amazing readers, without whom this would not be possible, thank you for all your kind words and continued support throughout all my endeavors and for taking this clean eating journey with me.

To Meg and my team at Callisto Media: Thank you for all your time and patience throughout this entire process, and for your constant encouragement. I am so happy to be part of the Callisto family.

about the author

Kenzie Swanhart is a food blogger and author of *Paleo in 28*, *Spiralize It!*, and *Clean Eating Bowls*. In an effort to cultivate a balanced lifestyle, Kenzie embraced a whole food, clean eating lifestyle and taught herself how to cook delicious, healthy food at home. Even with a full-time job and a busy side business, Kenzie always aims to cook dinner during the week and wants to inspire other to do the same—because cooking a simple, flavorful meal only takes 5 ingredients and 30 minutes or less.

Kenzie and her fiancé, Julien, live in Boston with their dog, Charlie.

CPSIA information can be obtained
at www.ICGtesting.com
Printed in the USA
BVOW05s1737150617

486957BV00004B/8/P